The Crucible

and Related Readings

McDougal Littell

A HOUGHTON MIFFLIN COMPANY

Evanston, Illinois   Boston   Dallas

Acknowledgments

Marion Boyars Publishers Ltd.: "Conversation With an American Writer," from *Early Poems* by Yevgeny Yevtushenko. Published by Marion Boyars Publishers, London, New York.

Simon & Schuster Inc.: "Guilt," from *The Devil's Shadow* by Clifford Lindsey Alderman. Copyright © 1967 by Clifford Lindsey Alderman. Reprinted with the permission of Simon & Schuster Inc.

Adam Goodheart: "How To Spot a Witch" by Adam Goodheart, from *Civilization*, March/April 1995 issue. Adam Goodheart is an editor and a columnist at *Civilization*, the magazine of the Library of Congress. By permission of the author.

The Ohio State University Press: "Young Goodman Brown," from *Mosses from an Old Manse*, volume X of the Centenary Edition of the Works of Nathaniel Hawthorne. Copyright © 1974 by the Ohio State University Press. All rights reserved. Reprinted by permission.

Barricade Books Inc.: Excerpts from *God's Country: America in the Fifties* by J. Ronald Oakley. Copyright © 1990 by J. Ronald Oakley. Reprinted with permission of Barricade Books Inc.

Edna St. Vincent Millay Society: "Justice Denied in Massachusetts" by Edna St. Vincent Millay, from *Collected Poems*, published by HarperCollins. Copyright 1928, 1955 by Edna St. Vincent Millay and Norma Millay Ellis. Reprinted by permission of Elizabeth Barnett, literary executor.

Rosemary A. Thurber: "The Very Proper Gander," from *Fables for Our Time* by James Thurber, published by HarperCollins. Copyright 1940 James Thurber; Copyright © 1968 Rosemary A. Thurber.

Random House, Inc.: "The Piece of String," from *The Best Stories of Guy de Maupassant* by Guy de Maupassant, edited by Saxe Commins. Copyright 1945 by Random House, Inc. Reprinted by permission of the Modern Library, a division of Random House, Inc.

The Crucible by Arthur Miller. Copyright 1952, 1953, 1954, renewed © 1980 by Arthur Miller. Used by permission of Viking Penguin, a division of Penguin Books USA Inc.

Cover illustration by Curtis Parker.
Author photo: AP/Wide World Photos.

Contents

Continued

The Crucible

Arthur Miller

Act One

....

(an overture)

(*A small upper bedroom in the home of* Reverend Samuel Parris, *Salem, Massachusetts, in the spring of the year 1692.*)

(*There is a narrow window at the left. Through its leaded panes the morning sunlight streams. A candle still burns near the bed, which is at the right. A chest, a chair, and a small table are the other furnishings. At the back a door opens on the landing of the stairway to the ground floor. The room gives off an air of clean spareness. The roof rafters are exposed, and the wood colors are raw and unmellowed.*)

(*As the curtain rises,* Reverend Parris *is discovered kneeling beside the bed, evidently in prayer. His daughter,* Betty Parris, *aged ten, is lying on the bed, inert.*)

At the time of these events Parris was in his middle forties. In history he cut a villainous path, and there is very little good to be said for him. He believed he was being persecuted wherever he went, despite his best efforts to win people and God to his side. In meeting, he felt insulted if someone rose to shut the door without first asking his permission. He was a widower with no interest in children, or talent with them. He regarded them as young adults, and until this strange crisis he, like the rest of Salem, never conceived that the children were anything but thankful for being permitted to walk straight, eyes slightly lowered, arms at the sides, and mouths shut until bidden to speak.

His house stood in the "town"—but we today would hardly call it a village. The meeting house was nearby, and from this point outward—toward the bay or inland —there were a few small-windowed, dark houses snuggling against the raw Massachusetts winter. Salem had been established hardly forty years before. To the European world the whole province was a barbaric frontier inhabited by a sect of fanatics who, nevertheless, were shipping out products of slowly increasing quantity and value.

No one can really know what their lives were like. They had no novelists—and would not have permitted anyone to read a novel if one were handy. Their creed forbade anything resembling a theater or "vain enjoyment." They did not celebrate Christmas, and a holiday from work meant only that they must concentrate even more upon prayer.

Which is not to say that nothing broke into this strict and somber way of life. When a new farmhouse was built, friends assembled to "raise the roof," and there would be special foods cooked and probably some potent cider passed around. There was a good supply of ne'er-do-wells in Salem, who dallied at the shovelboard in Bridget Bishop's tavern. Probably more than the creed, hard work kept the morals of the place from spoiling, for the people were forced to fight the land like heroes for every grain of corn, and no man had very much time for fooling around.

That there were some jokers, however, is indicated by the practice of appointing a two-man patrol whose duty was to "walk forth in the time of God's worship to take notice of such as either lye about the meeting house, without attending to the word and ordinances, or that lye at home or in the fields without giving good account thereof, and to take the names of such persons, and to present them to the magistrates, whereby they may be accordingly proceeded against." This predilection for minding other people's business was time-honored among the people of Salem, and it undoubtedly created many of the suspicions which were to feed the coming madness. It was also, in my opinion, one of the things that a John Proctor would rebel against, for the time of the armed camp had almost passed, and since the country was reasonably—although not wholly—safe, the old disciplines were beginning to rankle. But, as in all such matters, the issue was not clear-cut, for danger was still a possibility, and in unity still lay the best promise of safety.

The edge of the wilderness was close by. The American continent stretched endlessly west, and it was full of mystery for them. It stood, dark and threatening, over their shoulders night and day, for out of it Indian tribes marauded from time to time, and Reverend Parris had parishioners who had lost relatives to these heathen.

The parochial snobbery of these people was partly responsible for their failure to convert the Indians. Probably they also preferred to take land from heathens rather than from fellow Christians. At any rate, very few Indians were converted, and the Salem folk believed that the virgin forest was the Devil's last preserve, his home base and the citadel of his final stand. To the best of their knowledge the American forest was the last place on earth that was not paying homage to God.

For these reasons, among others, they carried about an air of innate resistance, even of persecution. Their fathers had, of course, been persecuted in England. So now they and their church found it necessary to deny any other sect its freedom, lest their New Jerusalem be defiled and corrupted by wrong ways and deceitful ideas.

They believed, in short, that they held in their steady hands the candle that would light the world. We have inherited this belief, and it has helped and hurt us. It helped them with the discipline it gave them. They were a dedicated folk, by and large, and they had to be to survive the life they had chosen or been born into in this country.

The proof of their belief's value to them may be taken from the opposite character of the first Jamestown settlement, farther south, in Virginia. The Englishmen who landed there were motivated mainly by a hunt for profit. They had thought to pick off the wealth of the new country and then return rich to England. They were a band of individualists, and a much more ingratiating group than the Massachusetts men. But Virginia destroyed them. Massachusetts tried to kill off the Puritans, but they combined; they set up a communal society which, in the beginning, was little more than an armed camp with an autocratic and very devoted leadership. It was, however, an autocracy by consent, for they were united from top to bottom by a commonly held ideology whose perpetuation was the reason and justification for all their sufferings. So their self-denial, their purposefulness, their suspicion of all vain pursuits, their hardhanded justice, were altogether perfect instruments for the conquest of this space so antagonistic to man.

But the people of Salem in 1692 were not quite the dedicated folk that arrived on the *Mayflower*. A vast differentiation had taken place, and in their own time a revolution had unseated the royal government and substituted a junta which was at this moment in power. The times, to their eyes, must have been out of joint, and to the common folk must have seemed as insoluble and complicated as do ours today. It is not hard to see how easily many could have been led to believe that the time of confusion had been brought upon them by deep and darkling forces. No hint of such speculation appears on the court record, but social disorder in any age breeds such mystical suspicions, and when, as in

Salem, wonders are brought forth from below the social surface, it is too much to expect people to hold back very long from laying on the victims with all the force of their frustrations.

The Salem tragedy, which is about to begin in these pages, developed from a paradox. It is a paradox in whose grip we still live, and there is no prospect yet that we will discover its resolution. Simply, it was this: for good purposes, even high purposes, the people of Salem developed a theocracy, a combine of state and religious power whose function was to keep the community together, and to prevent any kind of disunity that might open it to destruction by material or ideological enemies. It was forged for a necessary purpose and accomplished that purpose. But all organization is and must be grounded on the idea of exclusion and prohibition, just as two objects cannot occupy the same space. Evidently the time came in New England when the repressions of order were heavier than seemed warranted by the dangers against which the order was organized. The witch-hunt was a perverse manifestation of the panic which set in among all classes when the balance began to turn toward greater individual freedom.

When one rises above the individual villainy displayed, one can only pity them all, just as we shall be pitied someday. It is still impossible for man to organize his social life without repressions, and the balance has yet to be struck between order and freedom.

The witch-hunt was not, however, a mere repression. It was also, and as importantly, a long overdue opportunity for everyone so inclined to express publicly his guilt and sins, under the cover of accusations against the victims. It suddenly became possible—and patriotic and holy—for a man to say that Martha Corey had come into his bedroom at night, and that, while his wife was sleeping at his side, Martha laid herself down on his chest and "nearly suffocated him." Of course it was her spirit only, but his satisfaction at confessing himself was no lighter than if it had been Martha herself. One could not ordinarily speak such things in public.

Long-held hatreds of neighbors could now be openly expressed, and vengeance taken, despite the Bible's charitable injunctions. Land-lust which had been expressed before by constant bickering over boundaries and deeds, could now be elevated to the arena of morality; one could cry witch against one's neighbor and feel perfectly justified in the bargain. Old scores could be settled on a plane of heavenly combat between Lucifer and the Lord; suspicions and the envy of the miserable toward the happy could and did burst out in the general revenge.

(Reverend Parris *is praying now, and, though we cannot hear his words, a sense of his confusion hangs about him. He mumbles, then seems about to weep; then he weeps, then prays again; but his daughter does not stir on the bed.*)

(*The door opens, and his Negro slave enters.* Tituba *is in her forties.* Parris *brought her with him from Barbados, where he spent some years as a merchant before entering the ministry. She enters as one does who can no longer bear to be barred from the sight of her beloved, but she is also very frightened because her slave sense has warned her that, as always, trouble in this house eventually lands on her back.*)

Tituba (*already taking a step backward*). My Betty be hearty soon?

Parris. Out of here!

Tituba (*backing to the door*). My Betty not goin' die . . .

Parris (*scrambling to his feet in a fury*). Out of my sight! (*She is gone.*) Out of my—(*He is overcome with sobs. He clamps his teeth against them and closes the door and* *leans against it, exhausted.*) Oh, my God! God help me! (*Quaking with fear, mumbling to himself through his sobs, he goes to the bed and gently takes Betty's hand.*) Betty. Child. Dear child. Will you wake, will you open up your eyes! Betty, little one . . .

(*He is bending to kneel again when his niece,* Abigail Williams, *seventeen, enters—a strikingly beautiful girl, an orphan, with an endless capacity for dissembling. Now she is all worry and apprehension and propriety.*)

Abigail. Uncle? (*He looks to her.*) Susanna Walcott's here from Doctor Griggs.

Parris. Oh? Let her come, let her come.

Abigail (*leaning out the door to call to* Susanna, *who is down the hall a few steps*). Come in, Susanna.

(Susanna Walcott, *a little younger than* Abigail, *a nervous, hurried girl, enters.*)

Parris (*eagerly*). What does the doctor say, child?

Susanna (*craning around* Parris *to get a look at* Betty). He bid me come and tell you, reverend sir, that he cannot discover no medicine for it in his books.

Parris. Then he must search on.

Susanna. Aye, sir, he have been searchin' his books since he left you, sir. But he bid me tell you, that you might look to unnatural things for the cause of it.

Parris (*his eyes going wide*). No—no. There be no unnatural cause here. Tell him I have sent for Reverend Hale of Beverly, and Mr. Hale will surely confirm that. Let him look to medicine and put out all thought of unnatural causes here. There be none.

Susanna. Aye, sir. He bid me tell you. She turns to go.

Abigail. Speak nothin' of it in the village, Susanna.

Parris. Go directly home and speak nothing of unnatural causes.

Susanna. Aye, sir. I pray for her. (*She goes out.*)

Abigail. Uncle, the rumor of witchcraft is all about; I think you'd best go down and deny it yourself. The parlor's packed with people, sir. I'll sit with her.

Parris (*pressed, turns on her*). And what shall I say to them? That my daughter and my niece I discovered dancing like heathen in the forest?

Abigail. Uncle, we did dance; let you tell them I confessed it—and I'll be whipped if I must be. But they're speakin' of witchcraft. Betty's not witched.

Parris. Abigail, I cannot go before the congregation when I know you have not opened with me. What did you do with her in the forest?

Abigail. We did dance, uncle, and when you leaped out of the bush so suddenly, Betty was frightened and then she fainted. And there's the whole of it.

Parris Child. Sit you down.

Abigail (*quavering, as she sits*). I would never hurt Betty. I love her dearly.

Parris. Now look you, child, your punishment will come in its time. But if you trafficked with spirits in the forest I must know it now, for surely my enemies will, and they will ruin me with it.

Abigail. But we never conjured spirits.

Parris. Then why can she not move herself since midnight? This child is desperate! (Abigail *lowers her eyes.*) It must come out—my enemies will bring it out. Let me know what you done there. Abigail, do you understand that I have many enemies?

Abigail. I have heard of it, uncle.

Parris. There is a faction that is sworn to drive me from my pulpit. Do you understand that?

Abigail. I think so, sir.

Parris. Now then, in the midst of such disruption, my own household is discovered to be the very center of some obscene practice. Abominations are done in the forest—

Abigail. It were sport, uncle!

Parris (*pointing at* Betty). You call this sport? (*She lowers her eyes. He pleads*). Abigail, if you know something that may help the doctor, for God's sake tell it to me. (*She is silent.*) I saw Tituba waving her arms over the fire when I came on you. Why was she doing that? And I heard a screeching and gibberish coming from her mouth. She were swaying like a dumb beast over that fire!

Abigail. She always sings her Barbados songs, and we dance.

Parris. I cannot blink what I saw, Abigail, for my enemies will not blink it. I saw a dress lying on the grass.

Abigail (*innocently*). A dress?

Parris (*it is very hard to say*). Aye, a dress. And I thought I saw—someone naked running through the trees!

Abigail (*in terror*). No one was naked! You mistake yourself, uncle!

Parris (*with anger*). I saw it! (*He moves from her. Then, resolved*). Now tell me true, Abigail. And I pray you feel the weight of truth upon you, for now my ministry's at stake, my ministry and perhaps your cousin's life. Whatever abomination you have done, give me all of it now, for I dare not be taken unaware when I go before them down there.

Abigail. There is nothin' more. I ṣwear it, uncle.

Parris (*studies her, then nods, half convinced*). Abigail, I have fought here three long years to bend these stiff-necked people to me, and now, just now when some good respect is rising for me in the parish, you compromise my very character. I have given you a home, child, I have put clothes upon your back—now give me upright answer. Your name in the town—it is entirely white, is it not?

Abigail (*with an edge of resentment*). Why, I am sure it is, sir. There be no blush about my name.

Parris (*to the point*). Abigail, is there any other cause than you have told me, for your being discharged from Goody Proctor's service? I have heard it said, and I tell you as I heard it, that she comes so rarely to the church this year for she will not sit so close to something soiled. What signified that remark?

Abigail. She hates me, uncle, she must, for I would not be her slave. It's a bitter woman, a lying, cold, sniveling woman, and I will not work for such a woman!

Parris. She may be. And yet it has troubled me that you are now seven month out of their house, and in all this time no other family has ever called for your service.

Abigail. They want slaves, not such as I. Let them send to Barbados for that. I will not black my face for any of them! (*With ill-concealed resentment at him.*) Do you begrudge my bed, uncle?

Parris. No—no.

Abigail (*in a temper*). My name is good in the village! I will not have it said my name is soiled! Goody Proctor is a gossiping liar!

(*Enter* Mrs. Ann Putnam. *She is a twisted soul of forty-five, a death-ridden woman, haunted by dreams.*)

Parris (*as soon as the door begins to open*). No—no, I cannot have anyone. (*He sees her, and a certain deference springs into him, although his worry remains.*) Why, Goody Putnam, come in.

Mrs. Putnam (*full of breath, shiny-eyed*). It is a marvel. It is surely a stroke of hell upon you.

Parris. No, Goody Putnam, it is—

Mrs. Putnam (*glancing at* Betty). How high did she fly, how high?

Parris. No, no, she never flew—

Mrs. Putnam (*very pleased with it*). Why, it's sure she did. Mr. Collins saw her goin' over Ingersoll's barn, and come down light as bird, he says!

Parris. Now, look you, Goody Putnam, she never— (*Enter* Thomas Putnam, *a well-to-do, hard-handed landowner, near fifty.*) Oh, good morning, Mr. Putnam.

Putnam. It is a providence the thing is out now! It is a providence. (*He goes directly to the bed.*)

Parris. What's out, sir, what's—?

(Mrs. Putnam *goes to the bed.*)

Putnam (*looking down at* Betty). Why, her eyes is closed! Look you, Ann.

Mrs. Putnam. Why, that's strange. (*To* Parris). Ours is open.

Parris (*shocked*). Your Ruth is sick?

Mrs. Putnam (*with vicious certainty*). I'd not call it sick; the Devil's touch is heavier than sick. It's death, y'know, it's death drivin' into them, forked and hoofed.

Parris. Oh, pray not! Why, how does Ruth ail?

Mrs. Putnam. She ails as she must—she never waked this morning, but her eyes open and she walks, and hears naught, sees naught, and cannot eat. Her soul is taken, surely.

(Parris *is struck.*)

Putnam (*as though for further details*). They say you've sent for Reverend Hale of Beverly?

Parris (*with dwindling conviction now*). A precaution only. He has much experience in all demonic arts, and I—

Mrs. Putnam. He has indeed; and found a witch in Beverly last year, and let you remember that.

Parris. Now, Goody Ann, they only thought that were a witch, and I am certain there be no element of witchcraft here.

Putnam. No witchcraft! Now look you, Mr. Parris—

Parris. Thomas, Thomas, I pray you, leap not to witch-craft. I know that you—you least of all, Thomas, would ever wish so disastrous a charge laid upon me. We cannot leap to witchcraft. They will howl me out of Salem for such corruption in my house.

A word about Thomas Putnam. He was a man with many grievances, at least one of which appears justified. Some time before, his wife's brother-in-law, James Bayley, had been turned down as minister of Salem. Bayley had all the qualifications, and a two-thirds vote into the bargain, but a faction stopped his accep-tance, for reasons that are not clear.

Thomas Putnam was the eldest son of the richest man in the village. He had fought the Indians at Narragansett, and was deeply interested in parish affairs. He undoubtedly felt it poor payment that the village should so blatantly disregard his candidate for one of its more important offices, especially since he regarded himself as the intellectual superior of most of the people around him.

His vindictive nature was demonstrated long before the witchcraft began. Another former Salem minister, George Burroughs, had had to borrow money to pay for his wife's funeral, and, since the parish was remiss in his salary, he was soon bankrupt. Thomas and his brother John had Burroughs jailed for debts the man did not owe. The incident is important only in that Burroughs succeeded in becoming minister where Bayley, Thomas Putnam's brother-in-law, had been rejected; the motif of resentment is clear here. Thomas Putnam felt that his own name and the honor of his family had been smirched by the village, and he meant to right matters however he could.

Another reason to believe him a deeply embittered man was his attempt to break his father's will, which left a disproportionate amount to a stepbrother. As with every other public cause in which he tried to force his way, he failed in this.

So it is not surprising to find that so many accusations against people are in the handwriting of Thomas Putnam, or that his name is so often found as a witness corroborating the supernatural testimony, or that his daughter led the crying-out at the most opportune junctures of the trials, especially when— But we'll speak of that when we come to it.

Putnam (*at the moment he is intent upon getting* Parris, *for whom he has only contempt, to move toward the abyss*).
Mr. Parris, I have taken your part in all contention

here, and I would continue; but I cannot if you hold back in this. There are hurtful, vengeful spirits layin' hands on these children.

Parris. But, Thomas, you cannot—

Putnam. Ann! Tell Mr. Parris what you have done.

Mrs. Putnam. Reverend Parris, I have laid seven babies unbaptized in the earth. Believe me, sir, you never saw more hearty babies born. And yet, each would wither in my arms the very night of their birth. I have spoke nothin', but my heart has clamored intimations. And now, this year, my Ruth, my only —I see her turning strange. A secret child she has become this year, and shrivels like a sucking mouth were pullin' on her life too. And so I thought to send her to your Tituba—

Parris. To Tituba! What may Tituba—?

Mrs. Putnam. Tituba knows how to speak to the dead, Mr. Parris.

Parris. Goody Ann, it is a formidable sin to conjure up the dead!

Mrs. Putnam. I take it on my soul, but who else may surely tell us what person murdered my babies?

Parris (*horrified*). Woman!

Mrs. Putnam. They were murdered, Mr. Parris! And mark this proof! Mark it! Last night my Ruth were ever so close to their little spirits; I know it, sir. For how else is she struck dumb now except some power of darkness would stop her mouth? It is a marvelous sign, Mr. Parris!

Putnam. Don't you understand it, sir? There is a murdering witch among us, bound to keep herself in the dark. (Parris *turns to* Betty, *a frantic terror rising* *in him.*) Let your enemies make of it what they will, you cannot blink it more.

Parris (*to* Abigail). Then you were conjuring spirits last night.

Abigail (*whispering*). Not I, sir—Tituba and Ruth.

Parris (*turns now, with new fear, and goes to* Betty, *looks down at her, and then, gazing off*). Oh, Abigail, what proper payment for my charity! Now I am undone.

Putnam. You are not undone! Let you take hold here. Wait for no one to charge you—declare it yourself. You have discovered witchcraft—

Parris. In my house? In my house, Thomas? They will topple me with this! They will make of it a—

(*Enter* Mercy Lewis, *the Putnams' servant, a fat, sly, merciless girl of eighteen.*)

Mercy. Your pardons. I only thought to see how Betty is.

Putnam. Why aren't you home? Who's with Ruth?

Mercy. Her grandma come. She's improved a little, I think—she give a powerful sneeze before.

Mrs. Putnam. Ah, there's a sign of life!

Mercy. I'd fear no more, Goody Putnam. It were a grand sneeze; another like it will shake her wits together, I'm sure. (*She goes to the bed to look.*)

Parris. Will you leave me now, Thomas? I would pray a while alone.

Abigail. Uncle, you've prayed since midnight. Why do you not go down and—

Parris. No—no. (*To* Putnam). I have no answer for that crowd. I'll wait till Mr. Hale arrives. (*To get* Mrs. Putnam *to leave.*) If you will, Goody Ann . . .

Putnam. Now look you, sir. Let you strike out against the Devil, and the village will bless you for it! Come down, speak to them—pray with them. They're thirsting for your word, Mister! Surely you'll pray with them.

Parris (*swayed*). I'll lead them in a psalm, but let you say nothing of witchcraft yet. I will not discuss it. The cause is yet unknown. I have had enough contention since I came; I want no more.

Mrs. Putnam. Mercy, you go home to Ruth, d'y'hear?

Mercy. Aye, mum.

(Mrs. Putnam *goes out.*)

Parris (*to* Abigail). If she starts for the window, cry for me at once.

Abigail. I will, uncle.

Parris (*to* Putnam). There is a terrible power in her arms today. (*He goes out with* Putnam.)

Abigail (*with hushed trepidation*). How is Ruth sick?

Mercy. It's weirdish, I know not—she seems to walk like a dead one since last night.

Abigail (*turns at once and goes to* Betty, *and now, with fear in her voice*). Betty? (Betty *doesn't move. She shakes her.*) Now stop this! Betty! Sit up now!

(Betty *doesn't stir.* Mercy *comes over.*)

Mercy. Have you tried beatin' her? I gave Ruth a good one and it waked her for a minute. Here, let me have her.

Abigail (*holding* Mercy *back*). No, he'll be comin' up. Listen, now; if they be questioning us, tell them we danced—I told him as much already.

Mercy. Aye. And what more?

Abigail. He knows Tituba conjured Ruth's sisters to come out of the grave.

Mercy. And what more?

Abigail. He saw you naked.

Mercy (*clapping her hands together with a frightened laugh*). Oh, Jesus!

(*Enter* Mary Warren, *breathless. She is seventeen, a subservient, naive, lonely girl.*)

Mary Warren. What'll we do? The village is out! I just come from the farm; the whole country's talkin' witchcraft! They'll be callin' us witches, Abby!

Mercy (*pointing and looking at* Mary Warren). She means to tell, I know it.

Mary Warren. Abby, we've got to tell. Witchery's a hangin' error, a hangin' like they done in Boston two year ago! We must tell the truth, Abby! You'll only be whipped for dancin', and the other things!

Abigail. Oh, we'll be whipped!

Mary Warren. I never done none of it, Abby. I only looked!

Mercy (*moving menacingly toward* Mary). Oh, you're a great one for lookin', aren't you, Mary Warren? What a grand peeping courage you have!

(Betty, *on the bed, whimpers.* Abigail *turns to her at once.*)

Abigail. Betty? (*She goes to* Betty.) Now, Betty, dear, wake up now. It's Abigail. (*She sits* Betty *up and furiously shakes her.*) I'll beat you, Betty! (Betty *whimpers.*) My, you seem improving. I talked to your papa and I told him everything. So there's nothing to—

Betty (*darts off the bed, frightened of* Abigail, *and flattens herself against the wall*). I want my mama!

Abigail (*with alarm, as she cautiously approaches* Betty). What ails you, Betty? Your mama's dead and buried.

Betty. I'll fly to Mama. Let me fly! (*She raises her arms as though to fly, and streaks for the window, gets one leg out.*)

Abigail (*pulling her away from the window*). I told him everything; he knows now, he knows everything we—

Betty. You drank blood, Abby! You didn't tell him that!

Abigail. Betty, you never say that again! You will never—

Betty. You did, you did! You drank a charm to kill John Proctor's wife! You drank a charm to kill Goody Proctor!

Abigail (*smashes her across the face*). Shut it! Now shut it!

Betty (*collapsing on the bed*). Mama, Mama! (*She dissolves into sobs.*)

Abigail. Now look you. All of you. We danced. And Tituba conjured Ruth Putnam's dead sisters. And that is all. And mark this. Let either of you breathe a word, or the edge of a word, about the other things, and I will come to you in the black of some terrible night and I will bring a pointy reckoning that will shudder you. And you know I can do it; I saw Indians smash my dear parents' heads on the pillow next to mine, and I have seen some reddish work done at night, and I can make you wish you had never seen the sun go down! (*She goes to* Betty *and roughly sits her up.*) Now, you—sit up and stop this!

(*But* Betty *collapses in her hands and lies inert on the bed.*)

Mary Warren (*with hysterical fright*). What's got her? (Abigail *stares in fright at* Betty.) Abby, she's going to die! It's a sin to conjure, and we—

Abigail (*starting for* Mary). I say shut it, Mary Warren!

(*Enter* John Proctor. *On seeing him,* Mary Warren *leaps in fright.*)

Proctor was a farmer in his middle thirties. He need not have been a partisan of any faction in the town, but there is evidence to suggest that he had a sharp and biting way with hypocrites. He was the kind of man—powerful of body, even-tempered, and not easily led—who cannot refuse support to partisans without drawing their deepest resentment. In Proctor's presence a fool felt his foolishness instantly—and a Proctor is always marked for calumny therefore.

But as we shall see, the steady manner he displays does not spring from an untroubled soul. He is a sinner, a sinner not only against the moral fashion of the time, but against his own vision of decent conduct. These people had no ritual for the washing away of sins. It is another trait we inherited from them, and it has helped to discipline us as well as to breed hypocrisy among us. Proctor, respected and even feared in Salem, has come to regard himself as a kind of fraud. But no hint of this has yet appeared on the surface, and as he enters from the crowded parlor below it is a man in his prime we see, with a quiet confidence and an unexpressed, hidden force. Mary Warren, his servant, can barely speak for embarrassment and fear.

Mary Warren. Oh! I'm just going home, Mr. Proctor.

Proctor. Be you foolish, Mary Warren? Be you deaf? I forbid you leave the house, did I not? Why shall I pay you? I am looking for you more often than my cows!

Mary Warren. I only come to see the great doings in the world.

Proctor. I'll show you a great doin' on your arse one of these days. Now get you home; my wife is waitin' with your work! (*Trying to retain a shred of dignity, she goes slowly out.*)

Mercy Lewis (*both afraid of him and strangely titillated*). I'd best be off. I have my Ruth to watch. Good morning, Mr. Proctor.

(Mercy *sidles out. Since* Proctor's *entrance,* Abigail *has stood as though on tiptoe, absorbing his presence, wide-eyed. He glances at her, then goes to* Betty *on the bed.*)

Abigail. Gah! I'd almost forgot how strong you are, John Proctor!

Proctor (*looking at* Abigail *now, the faintest suggestion of a knowing smile on his face*). What's this mischief here?

Abigail (*with a nervous laugh*). Oh, she's only gone silly somehow.

Proctor. The road past my house is a pilgrimage to Salem all morning. The town's mumbling witchcraft.

Abigail. Oh, posh! (*Winningly she comes a little closer, with a confidential, wicked air.*) We were dancin' in the woods last night, and my uncle leaped in on us. She took fright, is all.

Proctor (*his smile widening*). Ah, you're wicked yet, aren't y'! (*A trill of expectant laughter escapes her, and she dares come closer, feverishly looking into his eyes.*) You'll be clapped in the stocks before you're twenty.

(*He takes a step to go, and she springs into his path.*)

Abigail. Give me a word, John. A soft word. (*Her concentrated desire destroys his smile.*)

Proctor. No, no, Abby. That's done with.

Abigail (*tauntingly*). You come five mile to see a silly girl fly? I know you better.

Proctor (*setting her firmly out of his path*). I come to see what mischief your uncle's brewin' now. (*With final emphasis.*) Put it out of mind, Abby.

Abigail (*grasping his hand before he can release her*). John —I am waitin' for you every night.

Proctor. Abby, I never give you hope to wait for me.

Abigail (*now beginning to anger—she can't believe it*). I have something better than hope, I think!

Proctor. Abby, you'll put it out of mind. I'll not be comin' for you more.

Abigail. You're surely sportin' with me.

Proctor. You know me better.

Abigail. I know how you clutched my back behind your house and sweated like a stallion whenever I come near! Or did I dream that? It's she put me out, you cannot pretend it were you. I saw your face when she put me out, and you loved me then and you do now!

Proctor. Abby, that's a wild thing to say—

Abigail. A wild thing may say wild things. But not so wild, I think. I have seen you since she put me out; I have seen you nights.

Proctor. I have hardly stepped off my farm this sevenmonth.

Abigail. I have a sense for heat, John, and yours has drawn me to my window, and I have seen you looking up, burning in your loneliness. Do you tell me you've never looked up at my window?

Proctor. I may have looked up.

Abigail (*now softening*). And you must. You are no wintry man. I know you, John. I *know* you. (*She is weeping.*) I cannot sleep for dreamin'; I cannot dream but I wake and walk about the house as though I'd find you comin' through some door. (*She clutches him desperately*).

Proctor (*gently pressing her from him, with great sympathy but firmly*). Child—

Abigail (*with a flash of anger*). How do you call me child!

Proctor. Abby, I may think of you softly from time to time. But I will cut off my hand before I'll ever reach for you again. Wipe it out of mind. We never touched, Abby.

Abigail. Aye, but we did.

Proctor. Aye, but we did not.

Abigail (*with a bitter anger*). Oh, I marvel how such a strong man may let such a sickly wife be—

Proctor (*angered—at himself as well*). You'll speak nothin' of Elizabeth!

Abigail. She is blackening my name in the village! She is telling lies about me! She is a cold, sniveling woman, and you bend to her! Let her turn you like a—

Proctor (*shaking her*). Do you look for whippin'?

(*A psalm is heard being sung below.*)

Abigail (*in tears*). I look for John Proctor that took me from my sleep and put knowledge in my heart! I never knew what pretense Salem was, I never knew the lying lessons I was taught by all these Christian women and their covenanted men! And now you bid me tear the light out of my eyes? I will not, I cannot! You loved me, John Proctor, and whatever sin it is, you love me yet! (*He turns abruptly to go out. She rushes to him.*) John, pity me, pity me!

(*The words "going up to Jesus" are heard in the psalm, and* Betty *claps her ears suddenly and whines loudly.*)

Abigail. Betty? (*She hurries to* Betty, *who is now sitting up and screaming.* Proctor *goes to* Betty *as* Abigail *is trying to pull her hands down, calling "Betty!"*)

Proctor (*growing unnerved*). What's she doing? Girl, what ails you? Stop that wailing!

(*The singing has stopped in the midst of this, and now Parris rushes in.*)

Parris. What happened? What are you doing to her? Betty! (*He rushes to the bed, crying, "Betty, Betty!"* Mrs. Putnam *enters, feverish with curiosity, and with her* Thomas Putnam *and* Mercy Lewis. Parris, *at the bed, keeps lightly slapping* Betty's *face, while she moans and tries to get up.*)

Abigail. She heard you singin' and suddenly she's up and screamin'.

Mrs. Putnam. The psalm! The psalm! She cannot bear to hear the Lord's name!

Parris. No. God forbid. Mercy, run to the doctor! Tell him what's happened here! (Mercy Lewis *rushes out.*)

Mrs. Putnam. Mark it for a sign, mark it!

(Rebecca Nurse, *seventy-two, enters. She is white-haired, leaning upon her walking-stick.*)

Putnam (*pointing at the whimpering* Betty). That is a notorious sign of witchcraft afoot, Goody Nurse, a prodigious sign!

Mrs. Putnam. My mother told me that! When they cannot bear to hear the name of—

Parris (*trembling*). Rebecca, Rebecca, go to her, we're lost. She suddenly cannot bear to hear the Lord's—

(Giles Corey, *eighty-three, enters. He is knotted with muscle, canny, inquisitive, and still powerful.*)

Rebecca. There is hard sickness here, Giles Corey, so please to keep the quiet.

Giles. I've not said a word. No one here can testify I've said a word. Is she going to fly again? I hear she flies.

Putnam. Man, be quiet now!

(*Everything is quiet.* Rebecca *walks across the room to the bed. Gentleness exudes from her.* Betty *is quietly whimpering, eyes shut.* Rebecca *simply stands over the child, who gradually quiets.*)

And while they are so absorbed, we may put a word in for Rebecca. Rebecca was the wife of Francis Nurse, who, from all accounts, was one of those men for whom both sides of the argument had to have respect. He was called upon to arbitrate disputes as though he were an unofficial judge, and Rebecca also enjoyed the high opinion most people had for him. By the time of the delusion, they had three hundred acres, and their children were settled in separate homesteads within the same estate. However, Francis had originally rented the land, and one theory has it that, as he gradually paid for it and raised his social status, there were those who resented his rise.

Another suggestion to explain the systematic campaign against Rebecca, and inferentially against Francis, is the land war he fought with his neighbors, one of whom was a Putnam. This squabble grew to the proportions of a battle in the woods between partisans of both sides, and it is said to have lasted for two days. As for Rebecca herself, the general opinion of her character was so high that to explain how anyone dared cry her out for a witch—and more, how adults could bring themselves to lay hands on her—we must look to the fields and boundaries of that time.

As we have seen, Thomas Putnam's man for the Salem ministry was Bayley. The Nurse clan had been in the faction that prevented Bayley's taking office. In addition, certain families allied to the Nurses by blood or friendship, and whose farms were contiguous with the Nurse farm or close to it, combined to break away from the Salem town authority and set up Topsfield, a new and independent entity whose existence was resented by old Salemites.

That the guiding hand behind the outcry was Putnam's is indicated by the fact that, as soon as it began, this Topsfield-Nurse faction absented themselves from church in protest and disbelief. It was Edward and Jonathan Putnam who signed the first complaint against Rebecca; and Thomas Putnam's little daughter was the one who fell into a fit at the hearing and pointed to Rebecca as her attacker. To top it all, Mrs. Putnam—who is now staring at the bewitched child on the bed—soon accused Rebecca's spirit of "tempting her to iniquity," a charge that had more truth in it than Mrs. Putnam could know.

Mrs. Putnam (astonished). What have you done?

(Rebecca, *in thought, now leaves the bedside and sits.*)

Parris (*wondrous and relieved*). What do you make of it, Rebecca?

Putnam (*eagerly*). Goody Nurse, will you go to my Ruth and see if you can wake her?

Rebecca (*sitting*). I think she'll wake in time. Pray calm yourselves. I have eleven children, and I am twenty-six times a grandma, and I have seen them all through their silly seasons, and when it come on them they will run the Devil bowlegged keeping up with their mischief. I think she'll wake when she tires of it. A child's spirit is like a child, you can never catch it by running after it; you must stand still, and, for love, it will soon itself come back.

Proctor. Aye, that's the truth of it, Rebecca.

Mrs. Putnam. This is no silly season, Rebecca. My Ruth is bewildered, Rebecca; she cannot eat.

Rebecca. Perhaps she is not hungered yet. (*To* Parris) I hope you are not decided to go in search of loose spirits, Mr. Parris. I've heard promise of that outside.

Parris. A wide opinion's running in the parish that the Devil may be among us, and I would satisfy them that they are wrong.

Proctor. Then let you come out and call them wrong. Did you consult the wardens before you called this minister to look for devils?

Parris. He is not coming to look for devils!

Proctor. Then what's he coming for?

Putnam. There be children dyin' in the village, Mister!

Proctor. I seen none dyin'. This society will not be a bag to swing around your head, Mr. Putnam. (*To* Parris) Did you call a meeting before you—?

Putnam. I am sick of meetings; cannot the man turn his head without he have a meeting?

Proctor. He may turn his head, but not to Hell!

Rebecca. Pray, John, be calm. (*Pause. He defers to her.*) Mr. Parris, I think you'd best send Reverend Hale back as soon as he come. This will set us all to arguin' again in the society, and we thought to have peace this year. I think we ought rely on the doctor now, and good prayer.

Mrs. Putnam. Rebecca, the doctor's baffled!

Rebecca. If so he is, then let us go to God for the cause of it. There is prodigious danger in the seeking of loose spirits. I fear it, I fear it. Let us rather blame ourselves and—

Putnam. How may we blame ourselves? I am one of nine sons; the Putnam seed have peopled this province. And yet I have but one child left of eight— and now she shrivels!

Rebecca. I cannot fathom that.

Mrs. Putnam (*with a growing edge of sarcasm*). But I must! You think it God's work you should never lose a child, nor grandchild either, and I bury all but one? There are wheels within wheels in this village, and fires within fires!

Putnam (*to* Parris). When Reverend Hale comes, you will proceed to look for signs of witchcraft here.

Proctor (*to* Putnam). You cannot command Mr. Parris. We vote by name in this society, not by acreage.

Putnam. I never heard you worried so on this society, Mr. Proctor. I do not think I saw you at Sabbath meeting since snow flew.

Proctor. I have trouble enough without I come five mile to hear him preach only hellfire and bloody damnation. Take it to heart, Mr. Parris. There are many others who stay away from church these days because you hardly ever mention God any more.

Parris (*now aroused*). Why, that's a drastic charge!

Rebecca. It's somewhat true; there are many that quail to bring their children—

Parris. I do not preach for children, Rebecca. It is not the children who are unmindful of their obligations toward this ministry.

Rebecca. Are there really those unmindful?

Parris. I should say the better half of Salem village—

Putnam. And more than that!

Parris. Where is my wood? My contract provides I be supplied with all my firewood. I am waiting since November for a stick, and even in November I had to show my frostbitten hands like some London beggar!

Giles. You are allowed six pound a year to buy your wood, Mr. Parris.

Parris. I regard that six pound as part of my salary. I am paid little enough without I spend six pound on firewood.

Proctor. Sixty, plus six for firewood—

Parris. The salary is sixty-six pound, Mr. Proctor! I am not some preaching farmer with a book under my arm; I am a graduate of Harvard College.

Giles. Aye, and well instructed in arithmetic!

Parris. Mr. Corey, you will look far for a man of my kind at sixty pound a year! I am not used to this poverty; I left a thrifty business in the Barbados to serve the Lord. I do not fathom it, why am I persecuted here? I cannot offer one proposition but there be a howling riot of argument. I have often wondered if the Devil be in it somewhere; I cannot understand you people otherwise.

Proctor. Mr. Parris, you are the first minister ever did demand the deed to this house—

Parris. Man! Don't a minister deserve a house to live in?

Proctor. To live in, yes. But to ask ownership is like you shall own the meeting house itself; the last meeting I were at you spoke so long on deeds and mortgages I thought it were an auction.

Parris. I want a mark of confidence, is all! I am your third preacher in seven years. I do not wish to be put out like the cat whenever some majority feels the whim. You people seem not to comprehend that a minister is the Lord's man in the parish; a minister is not to be so lightly crossed and contradicted—

Putnam. Aye!

Parris. There is either obedience or the church will burn like Hell is burning!

Proctor. Can you speak one minute without we land in Hell again? I am sick of Hell!

Parris. It is not for you to say what is good for you to hear!

Proctor. I may speak my heart, I think!

Parris (*in a fury*). What, are we Quakers? We are not Quakers here yet, Mr. Proctor. And you may tell that to your followers!

Proctor. My followers!

Parris (*now he's out with it*). There is a party in this church. I am not blind; there is a faction and a party.

Proctor. Against you?

Putnam. Against him and all authority!

Proctor. Why, then I must find it and join it.

(*There is shock among the others.*)

Rebecca. He does not mean that.

Putnam. He confessed it now!

Proctor. I mean it solemnly, Rebecca; I like not the smell of this "authority."

Rebecca. No, you cannot break charity with your minister. You are another kind, John. Clasp his hand, make your peace.

Proctor. I have a crop to sow and lumber to drag home. (*He goes angrily to the door and turns to* Corey *with a smile.*) What say you, Giles, let's find the party. He says there's a party.

Giles. I've changed my opinion of this man, John. Mr. Parris, I beg your pardon. I never thought you had so much iron in you.

Parris (*surprised*). Why, thank you, Giles!

Giles. It suggests to the mind what the trouble be among us all these years. (*To all*) Think on it. Wherefore is everybody suing everybody else? Think on it now, it's a deep thing, and dark as a pit. I have been six time in court this year—

Proctor (*familiarly, with warmth, although he knows he is approaching the edge of* Giles' *tolerance with this*). Is it the Devil's fault that a man cannot say you good morning without you clap him for defamation? You're old, Giles, and you're not hearin' so well as you did.

Giles (*he cannot be crossed*). John Proctor, I have only last month collected four pound damages for you publicly sayin' I burned the roof off your house, and I—

Proctor (*laughing*). I never said no such thing, but I've paid you for it, so I hope I can call you deaf without charge. Now come along, Giles, and help me drag my lumber home.

Putnam. A moment, Mr. Proctor. What lumber is that you're draggin', if I may ask you?

Proctor. My lumber. From out my forest by the riverside.

Putnam. Why, we are surely gone wild this year. What anarchy is this? That tract is in my bounds, it's in my bounds, Mr. Proctor.

Proctor. In your bounds! (*Indicating* Rebecca) I bought that tract from Goody Nurse's husband five months ago.

Putnam. He had no right to sell it. It stands clear in my grandfather's will that all the land between the river and—

Proctor. Your grandfather had a habit of willing land that never belonged to him, if I may say it plain.

Giles. That's God's truth; he nearly willed away my north pasture but he knew I'd break his fingers before he'd set his name to it. Let's get your lumber home, John. I feel a sudden will to work coming on.

Putnam. You load one oak of mine and you'll fight to drag it home!

Giles. Aye, and we'll win too, Putnam—this fool and I. Come on! (*He turns to* Proctor *and starts out.*)

Putnam. I'll have my men on you, Corey! I'll clap a writ on you!

(*Enter* Reverend John Hale *of Beverly.*)

Mr. Hale is nearing forty, a tight-skinned, eager-eyed intellectual. This is a beloved errand for him; on being called here to ascertain witchcraft he felt the pride of the specialist whose unique knowledge has at last been publicly called for. Like almost all men of learning, he spent a good deal of his time pondering the invisible world, especially since he had himself encountered a witch in his parish not long before. That woman, however, turned into a mere pest under his searching scrutiny, and the child she had allegedly been afflicting recovered her normal behavior after Hale had given her his kindness and a few days of rest in his own house. However, that experience never raised a doubt in his mind as to the reality of the underworld or the existence of Lucifer's many-faced lieutenants. And his belief is not to his discredit. Better minds than Hale's were—and still are—convinced that there is a society of spirits beyond our ken. One cannot help noting that one of his lines has never yet raised a laugh in any audience that has seen this play; it is his assurance that "We cannot look to superstition in this. The Devil is precise." Evidently we are not quite certain even now whether diabolism is holy and not to be scoffed at. And it is no accident that we should be so bemused.

Like Reverend Hale and the others on this stage, we conceive the Devil as a necessary part of a respectable view of cosmology. Ours is a divided empire in which certain ideas and emotions and actions are of God, and their opposites are of Lucifer. It is as impossible for most men to conceive of a morality without sin as of an earth without "sky." Since 1692 a great but superficial change has wiped out God's beard and the Devil's horns, but the world is still gripped between two diametrically opposed absolutes. The concept of unity, in which positive and negative are attributes of the same force, in which good and evil are relative, ever-changing, and always joined to the same phenomenon—such a concept is still reserved to the physical sciences and to the few who have grasped the history of ideas. When it is recalled that until the Christian era the underworld was never regarded as a hostile area, that all gods were useful and essentially friendly to man despite occasional lapses; when we see the steady and methodical inculcation into humanity of the idea of man's worthlessness—until redeemed— the necessity of the Devil may become evident as a weapon, a weapon designed and used time and time again in every age to whip men into a surrender to a particular church or church-state.

Our difficulty in believing the—for want of a better word—political inspiration of the Devil is due in great part to the fact that he is called up and damned not only by our social antagonists but by our own side, whatever it may be. The Catholic Church, through its Inquisition, is famous for cultivating Lucifer as the arch-fiend, but the Church's enemies relied no less upon the Old Boy to keep the human mind enthralled. Luther was himself accused of alliance with Hell, and he in turn accused his enemies. To complicate matters further, he believed that he had had contact with the Devil and had argued theology with him. I am not surprised at this, for at my own university a professor of history—a Lutheran, by the way—used to assemble his graduate students, draw the shades, and commune in the classroom with Erasmus. He was never, to my knowledge, officially scoffed at for this, the reason being that the university officials, like most of us, are the children of a history which still sucks at the Devil's teats. At this writing, only England has held back before the temptations of contemporary diabolism. In the countries of the Communist ideology, all resistance of any import is linked to the totally malign capitalist succubi, and in America any man who is not reactionary in his views is open to the charge of alliance with the Red hell. Political opposition, thereby, is given an inhumane overlay which then justifies the abrogation of all normally applied customs of civilized intercourse. A political policy is equated with moral right, and opposition to it with diabolical malevolence. Once such an equation is effectively made, society becomes a congerie of plots and counterplots, and the main role of government changes from that of the arbiter to that of the scourge of God.

The results of this process are no different now from what they ever were, except sometimes in the degree of cruelty inflicted, and not always even in that department. Normally the actions and deeds of a man were all that society felt comfortable in judging. The secret intent of an action was left to the ministers, priests, and rabbis to deal with. When diabolism rises, however, actions are the least important manifests of the true nature of a man. The Devil, as Reverend Hale said, is a wily one, and, until an hour before he fell, even God thought him beautiful in Heaven.

The analogy, however, seems to falter when one considers that, while there were no witches then, there are Communists and capitalists now, and in each camp there is certain proof that spies of each side are at work undermining the other. But this is a snobbish objection and not at all warranted by the facts. I have no doubt that people *were* communing with, and even worshiping, the Devil in Salem, and if the whole truth could be known in this case, as it is in others, we should discover a regular and conventionalized propitiation of the dark spirit. One certain evidence of this is the confession of Tituba, the slave of Reverend Parris, and another is the behavior of the children who were known to have indulged in sorceries with her.

There are accounts of similar *klatches* in Europe, where the daughters of the towns would assemble at night and, sometimes with fetishes, sometimes with a selected young man, give themselves to love, with some bastardly results. The Church, sharp-eyed as it must be when gods long dead are brought to life, condemned these orgies as witchcraft and interpreted them, rightly, as a resurgence of the Dionysiac forces it had crushed long before. Sex, sin, and the Devil were early linked, and so they continued to be in Salem, and are today. From all accounts there are no more puritanical mores in the world than those enforced by the Communists in Russia, where women's fashions, for instance, are as prudent and all-covering as any American Baptist would desire. The divorce laws lay a tremendous responsibility on the father for the care of his children. Even the laxity of divorce regulations in the early years of the revolution was undoubtedly a revulsion from the nineteenth-century Victorian immobility of marriage and the consequent hypocrisy that developed from it. If for no other reasons, a state so powerful, so jealous of the uniformity of its citizens, cannot long tolerate the atomization of the family. And yet, in American eyes at least, there remains the conviction that the Russian attitude toward women is lascivious. It is the Devil working again, just as he is working within the Slav who is shocked at the very idea of a woman's disrobing herself in a burlesque show. Our opposites are always robed in sexual sin, and it is from this unconscious conviction that demonology gains both its attractive sensuality and its capacity to infuriate and frighten.

Coming into Salem now, Reverend Hale conceives of himself much as a young doctor on his first call. His painfully acquired armory of symptoms, catchwords, and diagnostic procedures are now to be put to use at last. The road from Beverly is unusually busy this morning, and he has passed a hundred rumors that make him smile at the ignorance of the yeomanry in this most precise science. He feels himself allied with the best minds of Europe—kings, philosophers, scientists, and ecclesiasts of all churches. His goal is light, goodness and its preservation, and he knows the exaltation of the blessed whose intelligence, sharpened by minute examinations of enormous tracts, is finally called upon to face what may be a bloody fight with the Fiend himself.

(*He appears loaded down with half a dozen heavy books.*)

Hale. Pray you, someone take these!

Parris (*delighted*). Mr. Hale! Oh! it's good to see you again! (*Taking some books*) My, they're heavy!

Hale (*setting down his books*). They must be; they are weighted with authority.

Parris (*a little scared*). Well, you do come prepared!

Hale. We shall need hard study if it comes to tracking down the Old Boy. (*Noticing Rebecca*) You cannot be Rebecca Nurse?

Rebecca. I am, sir. Do you know me?

Hale. It's strange how I knew you, but I suppose you look as such a good soul should. We have all heard of your great charities in Beverly.

Parris. Do you know this gentleman? Mr. Thomas Putnam. And his good wife Ann.

Hale. Putnam! I had not expected such distinguished company, sir.

Putnam (*pleased*). It does not seem to help us today, Mr. Hale. We look to you to come to our house and save our child.

Hale. Your child ails too?

Mrs. Putnam. Her soul, her soul seems flown away. She sleeps and yet she walks . . .

Putnam. She cannot eat.

Hale. Cannot eat! (*Thinks on it. Then, to* Proctor *and* Giles Corey) Do you men have afflicted children?

Parris. No, no, these are farmers. John Proctor—

Giles Corey. He don't believe in witches.

Proctor (*to* Hale). I never spoke on witches one way or the other. Will you come, Giles?

Giles. No—no, John, I think not. I have some few queer questions of my own to ask this fellow.

Proctor. I've heard you to be a sensible man, Mr. Hale. I hope you'll leave some of it in Salem.

(Proctor *goes.* Hale *stands embarrassed for an instant.*)

Parris (*quickly*). Will you look at my daughter, sir? (*Leads* Hale *to the bed.*) She has tried to leap out the window; we discovered her this morning on the highroad, waving her arms as though she'd fly.

Hale (*narrowing his eyes*). Tries to fly.

Putnam. She cannot bear to hear the Lord's name, Mr. Hale; that's a sure sign of witchcraft afloat.

Hale (*holding up his hands*). No, no. Now let me instruct you. We cannot look to superstition in this. The Devil is precise; the marks of his presence are definite as stone, and I must tell you all that I shall not proceed unless you are prepared to believe me if I should find no bruise of hell upon her.

Parris. It is agreed, sir—it is agreed—we will abide by your judgment.

Hale. Good then. (*He goes to the bed, looks down at* Betty. *To* Parris) Now, sir, what were your first warning of this strangeness?

Parris. Why, sir—I discovered her—(*indicating* Abigail) and my niece and ten or twelve of the other girls, dancing in the forest last night.

Hale (*surprised*). You permit dancing?

Parris. No, no, it were secret—

Mrs. Putnam (*unable to wait*). Mr. Parris's slave has knowledge of conjurin', sir.

Parris (*to* Mrs. Putnam). We cannot be sure of that, Goody Ann—

Mrs. Putnam (*frightened, very softly*). I know it, sir. I sent my child—she should learn from Tituba who murdered her sisters.

Rebecca (*horrified*). Goody Ann! You sent a child to conjure up the dead?

Mrs. Putnam. Let God blame me, not you, not you, Rebecca! I'll not have you judging me any more! (*To* Hale) Is it a natural work to lose seven children before they live a day?

Parris. Sssh!

(Rebecca, *with great pain, turns her face away. There is a pause.*)

Hale. Seven dead in childbirth.

Mrs. Putnam (*softly*). Aye. (*Her voice breaks; she looks up at him. Silence.* Hale *is impressed.* Parris *looks to him. He goes to his books, opens one, turns pages, then reads. All wait, avidly.*)

Parris (*hushed*). What book is that?

Mrs. Putnam. What's there, sir?

Hale (*with a tasty love of intellectual pursuit*). Here is all the invisible world, caught, defined, and calculated. In these books the Devil stands stripped of all his brute disguises. Here are all your familiar spirits—your incubi and succubi; your witches that go by land, by air, and by sea; your wizards of the night and of the day. Have no fear now—we shall find him out if he has come among us, and I mean to crush him utterly if he has shown his face! (*He starts for the bed.*)

Rebecca. Will it hurt the child, sir?

Hale. I cannot tell. If she is truly in the Devil's grip we may have to rip and tear to get her free.

Rebecca. I think I'll go, then. I am too old for this. (*She rises.*)

Parris (*striving for conviction*). Why, Rebecca, we may open up the boil of all our troubles today!

Rebecca. Let us hope for that. I go to God for you, sir.

Parris (*with trepidation—and resentment*). I hope you do not mean we go to Satan here! (*Slight pause.*)

Rebecca. I wish I knew. (*She goes out; they feel resentful of her note of moral superiority.*)

Putnam (*abruptly*). Come, Mr. Hale, let's get on. Sit you here.

Giles. Mr. Hale, I have always wanted to ask a learned man—what signifies the readin' of strange books?

Hale. What books?

Giles. I cannot tell; she hides them.

Hale. Who does this?

Giles. Martha, my wife. I have waked at night many a time and found her in a corner, readin' of a book. Now what do you make of that?

Hale. Why, that's not necessarily—

Giles. It discomfits me! Last night—mark this—I tried and tried and could not say my prayers. And then she close her book and walks out of the house, and suddenly—mark this—I could pray again!

Old Giles must be spoken for, if only because his fate was to be so remarkable and so different from that of all the others. He was in his early eighties at this time, and was the most comical hero in the history. No man has ever been blamed for so much. If a cow was missed, the first thought was to look for her around Corey's house; a fire blazing up at night brought suspicion of arson to his door. He didn't give a hoot for public opinion, and only in his last years—after he had married Martha—did he bother much with the church. That she stopped his prayer is very probable, but he forgot to say that he'd only recently learned any prayers and it didn't take much to make him stumble over them. He was a crank and a nuisance, but withal a deeply innocent and brave man. In court once, he was asked if it were true that he had been frightened by the strange behavior of a hog and had then said he knew it to be the Devil in an animal's shape. "What frighted you?" he was asked. He forgot everything but the word "frighted," and instantly replied, "I do not know that I ever spoke that word in my life."

Hale. Ah! The stoppage of prayer—that is strange. I'll speak further on that with you.

Giles. I'm not sayin' she's touched the Devil, now, but I'd admire to know what books she reads and why she hides them. She'll not answer me, y' see.

Hale. Aye, we'll discuss it. (*To all*) Now mark me, if the Devil is in her you will witness some frightful wonders in this room, so please to keep your wits about you. Mr. Putnam, stand close in case she flies. Now, Betty, dear, will you sit up? (*Putnam comes in closer, ready-handed.* Hale *sits* Betty *up, but she hangs limp in his hands.*) Hmmm. (*He observes her carefully. The others watch breathlessly.*) Can you hear me? I am John Hale, minister of Beverly. I have come to help you, dear. Do you remember my two little girls in Beverly? (*She does not stir in his hands.*)

Parris (*in fright*). How can it be the Devil? Why would he choose my house to strike? We have all manner of licentious people in the village!

Hale. What victory would the Devil have to win a soul already bad? It is the best the Devil wants, and who is better than the minister?

Giles. That's deep, Mr. Parris, deep, deep!

Parris (*with resolution now*). Betty! Answer Mr. Hale! Betty!

Hale. Does someone afflict you, child? It need not be a woman, mind you, or a man. Perhaps some bird invisible to others comes to you—perhaps a pig, a mouse, or any beast at all. Is there some figure bids you fly? (*The child remains limp in his hands. In silence he lays her back on the pillow. Now, holding out his hands toward her, he intones*) In nomine Domini Sabaoth sui filiique ite ad infernos. (*She does not stir. He turns to* Abigail, *his eyes narrowing.*) Abigail, what sort of dancing were you doing with her in the forest?

Abigail. Why—common dancing is all.

Parris. I think I ought to say that I—I saw a kettle in the grass where they were dancing.

Abigail. That were only soup.

Hale. What sort of soup were in this kettle, Abigail?

Abigail. Why, it were beans—and lentils, I think, and—

Hale. Mr. Parris, you did not notice, did you, any living thing in the kettle? A mouse, perhaps, a spider, a frog—?

Parris (*fearfully*). I—do believe there were some movement—in the soup.

Abigail. That jumped in, we never put it in!

Hale (*quickly*). What jumped in?

Abigail. Why, a very little frog jumped—

Parris. A frog, Abby!

Hale (*grasping* Abigail). Abigail, it may be your cousin is dying. Did you call the Devil last night?

Abigail. I never called him! Tituba, Tituba . . .

Parris (*blanched*). She called the Devil?

Hale. I should like to speak with Tituba.

Parris. Goody Ann, will you bring her up? (Mrs. Putnam *exits.*)

Hale. How did she call him?

Abigail. I know not—she spoke Barbados.

Hale. Did you feel any strangeness when she called him? A sudden cold wind, perhaps? A trembling below the ground?

Abigail. I didn't see no Devil! (*Shaking* Betty) Betty, wake up. Betty! Betty!

Hale. You cannot evade me, Abigail. Did your cousin drink any of the brew in that kettle?

Abigail. She never drank it!

Hale. Did you drink it?

Abigail. No, sir!

Hale. Did Tituba ask you to drink it?

Abigail. She tried, but I refused.

Hale. Why are you concealing? Have you sold yourself to Lucifer?

Abigail. I never sold myself! I'm a good girl! I'm a proper girl!

(Mrs. Putnam *enters with* Tituba, *and instantly* Abigail *points at* Tituba.)

Abigail. She made me do it! She made Betty do it!

Tituba (*shocked and angry*). Abby!

Abigail. She makes me drink blood!

Parris. Blood!!

Mrs. Putnam. My baby's blood?

Tituba. No, no, chicken blood. I give she chicken blood!

Hale. Woman, have you enlisted these children for the Devil?

Tituba. No, no, sir, I don't truck with no Devil!

Hale. Why can she not wake? Are you silencing this child?

Tituba. I love me Betty!

Hale. You have sent your spirit out upon this child, have you not? Are you gathering souls for the Devil?

Abigail. She sends her spirit on me in church; she makes me laugh at prayer!

Parris. She have often laughed at prayer!

Abigail. She comes to me every night to go and drink blood!

Tituba. You beg me to conjure! She beg me make charm—

Abigail. Don't lie! (*To* Hale) She comes to me while I sleep; she's always making me dream corruptions!

Tituba. Why you say that, Abby?

Abigail. Sometimes I wake and find myself standing in the open doorway and not a stitch on my body! I always hear her laughing in my sleep. I hear her singing her Barbados songs and tempting me with—

Tituba. Mister Reverend, I never—

Hale (*resolved now*). Tituba, I want you to wake this child.

Tituba. I have no power on this child, sir.

Hale. You most certainly do, and you will free her from it now! When did you compact with the Devil?

Tituba. I don't compact with no Devil!

Parris. You will confess yourself or I will take you out and whip you to your death, Tituba!

Putnam. This woman must be hanged! She must be taken and hanged!

Tituba (*terrified, falls to her knees*). No, no, don't hang Tituba! I tell him I don't desire to work for him, sir.

Parris. The Devil?

Hale. Then you saw him! (Tituba *weeps*.) Now Tituba, I know that when we bind ourselves to Hell it is very hard to break with it. We are going to help you tear yourself free—

Tituba (*frightened by the coming process*). Mister Reverend, I do believe somebody else be witchin' these children.

Hale. Who?

Tituba. I don't know, sir, but the Devil got him numerous witches.

Hale. Does he! It is a clue. Tituba, look into my eyes. Come, look into me. (*She raises her eyes to his fearfully.*) You would be a good Christian woman, would you not, Tituba?

Tituba. Aye, sir, a good Christian woman.

Hale. And you love these little children?

Tituba. Oh, yes, sir, I don't desire to hurt little children.

Hale. And you love God, Tituba?

Tituba. I love God with all my bein'.

Hale. Now, in God's holy name—

Tituba. Bless Him. Bless Him. (*She is rocking on her knees, sobbing in terror.*)

Hale. And to His glory—

Tituba. Eternal glory. Bless Him—bless God . . .

Hale. Open yourself, Tituba—open yourself and let God's holy light shine on you.

Tituba. Oh, bless the Lord.

Hale. When the Devil comes to you does he ever come—with another person? (*She stares up into his face.*) Perhaps another person in the village? Someone you know.

Parris. Who came with him?

Putnam. Sarah Good? Did you ever see Sarah Good with him? Or Osburn?

Parris. Was it man or woman came with him?

Tituba. Man or woman. Was—was woman.

Parris. What woman? A woman, you said. What woman?

Tituba. It was black dark, and I—

Parris. You could see him, why could you not see her?

Tituba. Well, they was always talking; they was always runnin' round and carryin' on—

Parris. You mean out of Salem? Salem witches?

Tituba. I believe so, yes, sir.

(*Now Hale takes her hand. She is surprised.*)

Hale. Tituba. You must have no fear to tell us who they are, do you understand? We will protect you.

The Devil can never overcome a minister. You know that, do you not?

Tituba (*kisses Hale's hand*). Aye, sir, oh, I do.

Hale. You have confessed yourself to witchcraft, and that speaks a wish to come to Heaven's side. And we will bless you, Tituba.

Tituba (*deeply relieved*). Oh, God bless you, Mr. Hale!

Hale (*with rising exaltation*). You are God's instrument put in our hands to discover the Devil's agents among us. You are selected, Tituba, you are chosen to help us cleanse our village. So speak utterly, Tituba, turn your back on him and face God—face God, Tituba, and God will protect you.

Tituba (*joining with him*). Oh, God, protect Tituba!

Hale (*kindly*). Who came to you with the Devil? Two? Three? Four? How many?

(Tituba *pants, and begins rocking back and forth again, staring ahead.*)

Tituba. There was four. There was four.

Parris (*pressing in on her*). Who? Who? Their names, their names!

Tituba (*suddenly bursting out*). Oh, how many times he bid me kill you, Mr. Parris!

Parris. Kill me!

Tituba (*in a fury*). He say Mr. Parris must be kill! Mr. Parris no goodly man, Mr. Parris mean man and no gentle man, and he bid me rise out of my bed and cut your throat! (*They gasp.*) But I tell him "No! I don't hate that man. I don't want kill that man." But he say, "You work for me, Tituba, and I make you free! I give you pretty dress to wear, and put you way high up in the air, and you gone fly back to Barbados!" And I say, "You lie, Devil, you lie!" And then he come one stormy night to me, and he say, "Look! I have white people belong to me." And I look—and there was Goody Good.

Parris. Sarah Good!

Tituba (*rocking and weeping*). Aye, sir, and Goody Osburn.

Mrs. Putnam. I knew it! Goody Osburn were midwife to me three times. I begged you, Thomas, did I not? I begged him not to call Osburn because I feared her. My babies always shriveled in her hands!

Hale. Take courage, you must give us all their names. How can you bear to see this child suffering? Look at her, Tituba. (*He is indicating* Betty *on the bed.*) Look at her God-given innocence; her soul is so tender; we must protect her, Tituba; the Devil is out and preying on her like a beast upon the flesh of the pure lamb. God will bless you for your help.

(Abigail *rises, staring as though inspired, and cries out.*)

Abigail. I want to open myself! (*They turn to her, startled. She is enraptured, as though in a pearly light.*) I want the light of God, I want the sweet love of Jesus! I danced for the Devil; I saw him; I wrote in his book; I go back to Jesus; I kiss His hand. I saw Sarah Good with the Devil! I saw Goody Osburn with the Devil! I saw Bridget Bishop with the Devil!

(*As she is speaking,* Betty *is rising from the bed, a fever in her eyes, and picks up the chant.*)

Betty (*staring too*). I saw George Jacobs with the Devil! I saw Goody Howe with the Devil!

Parris. She speaks! (*He rushes to embrace* Betty.) She speaks!

Hale. Glory to God! It is broken, they are free!

Betty (*calling out hysterically and with great relief*). I saw Martha Bellows with the Devil!

Abigail. I saw Goody Sibber with the Devil! (*It is rising to a great glee.*)

Putnam. The marshal, I'll call the marshal!

(Parris *is shouting a prayer of thanksgiving.*)

Betty. I saw Alice Barrow with the Devil!

(*The curtain begins to fall.*)

Hale (*as Putnam goes out*). Let the marshal bring irons!

Abigail. I saw Goody Hawkins with the Devil!

Betty. I saw Goody Bibber with the Devil!

Abigail. I saw Goody Booth with the Devil!

(*On their ecstatic cries*)

THE CURTAIN FALLS

Act Two

(*The common room of* Proctor's *house, eight days later.*)

(*At the right is a door opening on the fields outside. A fireplace is at the left, and behind it a stairway leading upstairs. It is the low, dark, and rather long living room of the time. As the curtain rises, the room is empty. From above,* Elizabeth *is heard softly singing to the children. Presently the door opens and* John Proctor *enters, carrying his gun. He glances about the room as he comes toward the fireplace, then halts for an instant as he hears her singing. He continues on to the fireplace, leans the gun against the wall as he swings a pot out of the fire and smells it. Then he lifts out the ladle and tastes. He is not quite pleased. He reaches to a cupboard, takes a pinch of salt, and drops it into the pot. As he is tasting again, her footsteps are heard on the stair. He swings the pot into the fireplace and goes to a basin and washes his hands and face.* Elizabeth *enters.*)

Elizabeth. What keeps you so late? It's almost dark.

Proctor. I were planting far out to the forest edge.

Elizabeth. Oh, you're done then.

Proctor. Aye, the farm is seeded. The boys asleep?

Elizabeth. They will be soon. (*And she goes to the fireplace, proceeds to ladle up stew in a dish.*)

Proctor. Pray now for a fair summer.

Elizabeth. Aye.

Proctor. Are you well today?

Elizabeth. I am. (*She brings the plate to the table, and, indicating the food*) It is a rabbit.

Proctor (*going to the table*). Oh, is it! In Jonathan's trap?

Elizabeth. No, she walked into the house this afternoon; I found her sittin' in the corner like she come to visit.

Proctor. Oh, that's a good sign walkin' in.

Elizabeth. Pray God. It hurt my heart to strip her, poor rabbit. (*She sits and watches him taste it.*)

Proctor. It's well seasoned.

Elizabeth (*blushing with pleasure*). I took great care. She's tender?

Proctor. Aye. (*He eats. She watches him.*) I think we'll see green fields soon. It's warm as blood beneath the clods.

Elizabeth. That's well.

(Proctor *eats, then looks up.*)

Proctor. If the crop is good I'll buy George Jacob's heifer. How would that please you?

Elizabeth. Aye, it would.

Proctor (*with a grin*). I mean to please you, Elizabeth.

Elizabeth (*it is hard to say*). I know it, John.

(*He gets up, goes to her, kisses her. She receives it. With a certain disappointment, he returns to the table.*)

Proctor (*as gently as he can*). Cider?

Elizabeth (*with a sense of reprimanding herself for having forgot*). Aye! (*She gets up and goes and pours a glass for him. He now arches his back.*)

Proctor. This farm's a continent when you go foot by foot droppin' seeds in it.

Elizabeth (*coming with the cider*). It must be.

Proctor (*drinks a long draught, then, putting the glass down*). You ought to bring some flowers in the house.

Elizabeth. Oh! I forgot! I will tomorrow.

Proctor. It's winter in here yet. On Sunday let you come with me, and we'll walk the farm together; I never see such a load of flowers on the earth. (*With good feeling he goes and looks up at the sky through the open doorway.*) Lilacs have a purple smell. Lilac is the smell of night-fall, I think. Massachusetts is a beauty in the spring!

Elizabeth. Aye, it is.

(*There is a pause. She is watching him from the table as he stands there absorbing the night. It is as though she would speak but cannot. Instead, now, she takes up his plate and glass and fork and goes with them to the basin. Her back is turned to him. He turns to her and watches her. A sense of their separation rises.*)

Proctor. I think you're sad again. Are you?

Elizabeth (*she doesn't want friction, and yet she must*). You come so late I thought you'd gone to Salem this afternoon.

Proctor. Why? I have no business in Salem.

Elizabeth. You did speak of going, earlier this week.

Proctor (*he knows what she means*). I thought better of it since.

Elizabeth. Mary Warren's there today.

Proctor. Why'd you let her? You heard me forbid her go to Salem any more!

Elizabeth. I couldn't stop her.

Proctor (*holding back a full condemnation of her*). It is a fault, it is a fault, Elizabeth—you're the mistress here, not Mary Warren.

Elizabeth. She frightened all my strength away.

Proctor. How may that mouse frighten you, Elizabeth? You—

Elizabeth. It is a mouse no more. I forbid her go, and she raises up her chin like the daughter of a prince and says to me, "I must go to Salem, Goody Proctor; I am an official of the court!"

Proctor. Court! What court?

Elizabeth. Aye, it is a proper court they have now. They've sent four judges out of Boston, she says, weighty magistrates of the General Court, and at the head sits the Deputy Governor of the Province.

Proctor (*astonished*). Why, she's mad.

Elizabeth. I would to God she were. There be fourteen people in the jail now, she says. (*Proctor simply looks at her, unable to grasp it.*) And they'll be tried, and the court have power to hang them too, she says.

Proctor (*scoffing, but without conviction*). Ah, they'd never hang—

Elizabeth. The Deputy Governor promise hangin' if they'll not confess, John. The town's gone wild, I think. She speak of Abigail, and I thought she were a saint, to hear her. Abigail brings the other girls into the court, and where she walks the crowd will part like the sea for Israel. And folks are brought before them, and if they scream and howl and fall to the floor—the person's clapped in the jail for bewitchin' them.

Proctor (*wide-eyed*). Oh, it is a black mischief.

Elizabeth. I think you must go to Salem, John. (*He turns to her.*) I think so. You must tell them it is a fraud.

Proctor (*thinking beyond this*). Aye, it is, it is surely.

Elizabeth. Let you go to Ezekiel Cheever—he knows you well. And tell him what she said to you last week in her uncle's house. She said it had naught to do with witchcraft, did she not?

Proctor (*in thought*). Aye, she did, she did. (*Now, a pause.*)

Elizabeth (*quietly, fearing to anger him by prodding*). God forbid you keep that from the court, John. I think they must be told.

Proctor (*quietly, struggling with his thought*). Aye, they must, they must. It is a wonder they do believe her.

Elizabeth. I would go to Salem now, John—let you go tonight.

Proctor. I'll think on it.

Elizabeth (*with her courage now*). You cannot keep it, John.

Proctor (*angering*). I know I cannot keep it. I say I will think on it!

Elizabeth (*hurt, and very coldly*). Good, then, let you think on it. (*She stands and starts to walk out of the room.*)

Proctor. I am only wondering how I may prove what she told me, Elizabeth. If the girl's a saint now, I think it is not easy to prove she's fraud, and the town gone so silly. She told it to me in a room alone—I have no proof for it.

Elizabeth. You were alone with her?

Proctor (*stubbornly*). For a moment alone, aye.

Elizabeth. Why, then, it is not as you told me.

Proctor (*his anger rising*). For a moment, I say. The others come in soon after.

Elizabeth (*quietly—she has suddenly lost all faith in him*). Do as you wish, then. (*She starts to turn.*)

Proctor. Woman. (*She turns to him.*) I'll not have your suspicion any more.

Elizabeth (*a little loftily*). I have no—

Proctor. I'll not have it!

Elizabeth. Then let you not earn it.

Proctor (*with a violent undertone*). You doubt me yet?

Elizabeth (*with a smile, to keep her dignity*). John, if it were not Abigail that you must go to hurt, would you falter now? I think not.

Proctor. Now look you—

Elizabeth. I see what I see, John.

Proctor (*with solemn warning*). You will not judge me more, Elizabeth. I have good reason to think before I charge fraud on Abigail, and I will think on it. Let you look to your own improvement before you go to judge your husband any more. I have forgot Abigail, and—

Elizabeth. And I.

Proctor. Spare me! You forget nothin' and forgive nothin'. Learn charity, woman. I have gone tiptoe in this house all seven month since she is gone. I have not moved from there to there without I think to please you, and still an everlasting funeral marches round your heart. I cannot speak but I am doubted, every moment judged for lies, as though I come into a court when I come into this house!

Elizabeth. John, you are not open with me. You saw her with a crowd, you said. Now you—

Proctor. I'll plead my honesty no more, Elizabeth.

Elizabeth (*now she would justify herself*). John, I am only—

Proctor. No more! I should have roared you down when first you told me your suspicion. But I wilted, and, like a Christian, I confessed. Confessed! Some dream I had must have mistaken you for God that day. But you're not, you're not, and let you remember it! Let you look sometimes for the goodness in me, and judge me not.

Elizabeth. I do not judge you. The magistrate sits in your heart that judges you. I never thought you but a good man, John—(*with a smile*)—only somewhat bewildered.

Proctor (*laughing bitterly*). Oh, Elizabeth, your justice would freeze beer! (*He turns suddenly toward a sound outside. He starts for the door as* Mary Warren *enters. As soon as he sees her, he goes directly to her and grabs her by her cloak, furious.*) How do you go to Salem when I forbid it? Do you mock me? (*Shaking her.*) I'll whip you if you dare leave this house again!

(*Strangely, she doesn't resist him, but hangs limply by his grip.*)

Mary Warren. I am sick, I am sick, Mr. Proctor. Pray, pray, hurt me not. (*Her strangeness throws him off, and her evident pallor and weakness. He frees her.*) My insides are all shuddery; I am in the proceedings all day, sir.

Proctor (*with draining anger—his curiosity is draining it*). And what of these proceedings here? When will you proceed to keep this house, as you are paid nine pound a year to do—and my wife not wholly well?

(*As though to compensate,* Mary Warren *goes to* Elizabeth *with a small rag doll.*)

Mary Warren. I made a gift for you today, Goody Proctor. I had to sit long hours in a chair, and passed the time with sewing.

Elizabeth (*perplexed, looking at the doll*). Why, thank you, it's a fair poppet.

Mary Warren (*with a trembling, decayed voice*). We must all love each other now, Goody Proctor.

Elizabeth (*amazed at her strangeness*). Aye, indeed we must.

Mary Warren (*glancing at the room*). I'll get up early in the morning and clean the house. I must sleep now. (*She turns and starts off.*)

Proctor. Mary. (*She halts.*) Is it true? There be fourteen women arrested?

Mary Warren. No, sir. There be thirty-nine now—(*She suddenly breaks off and sobs and sits down, exhausted.*)

Elizabeth. Why, she's weepin'! What ails you, child?

Mary Warren. Goody Osburn—will hang!

(*There is a shocked pause, while she sobs.*)

Proctor. Hang! (*He calls into her face.*) Hang, y'say?

Mary Warren (*through her weeping*). Aye.

Proctor. The Deputy Governor will permit it?

Mary Warren. He sentenced her. He must. (*To ameliorate it.*) But not Sarah Good. For Sarah Good confessed, y'see.

Proctor. Confessed! To what?

Mary Warren. That she—(*in horror at the memory*)—she sometimes made a compact with Lucifer, and wrote her name in his black book—with her blood—and bound herself to torment Christians till God's thrown down—and we all must worship Hell forevermore.

(*Pause.*)

Proctor. But—surely you know what a jabberer she is. Did you tell them that?

Mary Warren. Mr. Proctor, in open court she near to choked us all to death.

Proctor. How, choked you?

Mary Warren. She sent her spirit out.

Elizabeth. Oh, Mary, Mary, surely you—

Mary Warren (*with an indignant edge*). She tried to kill me many times, Goody Proctor!

Elizabeth. Why, I never heard you mention that before.

Mary Warren. I never knew it before. I never knew anything before. When she come into the court I say to myself, I must not accuse this woman, for she sleep in ditches, and so very old and poor. But then—then she sit there, denying and denying, and I feel a misty coldness climbin' up my back, and the skin on my skull begin to creep, and I feel a clamp around my neck and I cannot breathe air; and then—(*entranced*)—I hear a voice, a screamin' voice, and it were my voice—and all at once I remembered everything she done to me!

Proctor. Why? What did she do to you?

Mary Warren (*like one awakened to a marvelous secret insight*). So many time, Mr. Proctor, she come to this very door, beggin' bread and a cup of cider—and mark this: whenever I turned her away empty, she mumbled.

Elizabeth. Mumbled! She may mumble if she's hungry.

Mary Warren. But *what* does she mumble? You must remember, Goody Proctor. Last month—a Monday, I think—she walked away, and I thought my guts would burst for two days after. Do you remember it?

Elizabeth. Why—I do, I think, but—

Mary Warren. And so I told that to Judge Hathorne, and he asks her so. "Sarah Good," says he, "what curse do you mumble that this girl must fall sick after turning you away?" (*And then she replies—mimicking an old crone*)—"Why, your excellence, no curse at all. I only say my commandments; I hope I may say my commandments," says she!

Elizabeth. And that's an upright answer.

Mary Warren. Aye, but then Judge Hathorne say, "Recite for us your commandments!"—(*leaning avidly toward them*)—and of all the ten she could not say a single one. She never knew no commandments, and they had her in a flat lie!

Proctor. And so condemned her?

Mary Warren (*now a little strained, seeing his stubborn doubt*). Why, they must when she condemned herself.

Proctor. But the proof, the proof!

Mary Warren (*with greater impatience with him*). I told you the proof. It's hard proof, hard as rock, the judges said.

Proctor (*pauses an instant, then*). You will not go to court again, Mary Warren.

Mary Warren. I must tell you, sir, I will be gone every day now. I am amazed you do not see what weighty work we do.

Proctor. What work you do! It's strange work for a Christian girl to hang old women!

Mary Warren. But, Mr. Proctor, they will not hang them if they confess. Sarah Good will only sit in jail some time—(*recalling*)—and here's a wonder for you; think on this. Goody Good is pregnant!

Elizabeth. Pregnant! Are they mad? The woman's near to sixty!

Mary Warren. They had Doctor Griggs examine her, and she's full to the brim. And smokin' a pipe all these years, and no husband either! But she's safe, thank God, for they'll not hurt the innocent child. But be that not a marvel? You must see it, sir, it's God's work we do. So I'll be gone every day for some time. I'm—I am an official of the court, they say, and I—(*She has been edging toward offstage.*)

Proctor. I'll official you! (*He strides to the mantel, takes down the whip hanging there.*)

Mary Warren (*terrified, but coming erect, striving for her authority*). I'll not stand whipping any more!

Elizabeth (*hurriedly, as Proctor approaches*). Mary, promise now you'll stay at home—

Mary Warren (*backing from him, but keeping her erect posture, striving, striving for her way*). The Devil's loose in Salem, Mr. Proctor; we must discover where he's hiding!

Proctor. I'll whip the Devil out of you! (*With whip raised he reaches out for her, and she streaks away and yells.*)

Mary Warren (*pointing at Elizabeth*). I saved her life today!

(*Silence. His whip comes down.*)

Elizabeth (*softly*). I am accused?

Mary Warren (*quaking*). Somewhat mentioned. But I said I never see no sign you ever sent your spirit out to hurt no one, and seeing I do live so closely with you, they dismissed it.

Elizabeth. Who accused me?

Mary Warren. I am bound by law, I cannot tell it. (*To Proctor*) I only hope you'll not be so sarcastical no more. Four judges and the King's deputy sat to dinner with us but an hour ago. I—I would have you speak civilly to me, from this out.

Proctor (*in horror, muttering in disgust at her*). Go to bed.

Mary Warren (*with a stamp of her foot*). I'll not be ordered to bed no more, Mr. Proctor! I am eighteen and a woman, however single!

Proctor. Do you wish to sit up? Then sit up.

Mary Warren. I wish to go to bed!

Proctor (*in anger*). Good night, then!

Mary Warren. Good night. (*Dissatisfied, uncertain of herself, she goes out. Wide-eyed, both,* Proctor *and* Elizabeth *stand staring.*)

Elizabeth (*quietly*). Oh, the noose, the noose is up!

Proctor. There'll be no noose.

Elizabeth. She wants me dead. I knew all week it would come to this!

Proctor (*without conviction*). They dismissed it. You heard her say—

Elizabeth. And what of tomorrow? She will cry me out until they take me!

Proctor. Sit you down.

Elizabeth. She wants me dead, John, you know it!

Proctor. I say sit down! (*She sits, trembling. He speaks quietly, trying to keep his wits.*) Now we must be wise, Elizabeth.

Elizabeth (*with sarcasm, and a sense of being lost*). Oh, indeed, indeed!

Proctor. Fear nothing. I'll find Ezekiel Cheever. I'll tell him she said it were all sport.

Elizabeth. John, with so many in the jail, more than Cheever's help is needed now, I think. Would you favor me with this? Go to Abigail.

Proctor (*his soul hardening as he senses . . .*). What have I to say to Abigail?

Elizabeth (*delicately*). John—grant me this. You have a faulty understanding of young girls. There is a promise made in any bed—

Proctor (*striving against his anger*). What promise!

Elizabeth. Spoke or silent, a promise is surely made. And she may dote on it now—I am sure she does— and thinks to kill me, then to take my place.

(Proctor's *anger is rising; he cannot speak.*)

Elizabeth. It is her dearest hope, John, I know it. There be a thousand names; why does she call mine? There be a certain danger in calling such a name— I am no Goody Good that sleeps in ditches, nor Osburn, drunk and half-witted. She'd dare not call out such a farmer's wife but there be monstrous profit in it. She thinks to take my place, John.

Proctor. She cannot think it! (*He knows it is true.*)

Elizabeth (*"reasonably"*). John, have you ever shown her somewhat of contempt? She cannot pass you in the church but you will blush—

Proctor. I may blush for my sin.

Elizabeth. I think she sees another meaning in that blush.

Proctor. And what see you? What see you, Elizabeth?

Elizabeth (*"conceding"*). I think you be somewhat ashamed, for I am there, and she so close.

Proctor. When will you know me, woman? Were I stone I would have cracked for shame this seven month!

Elizabeth. Then go and tell her she's a whore. Whatever promise she may sense—break it, John, break it.

Proctor (*between his teeth*). Good, then. I'll go. He starts for his rifle.

Elizabeth (*trembling, fearfully*). Oh, how unwillingly!

Proctor (*turning on her, rifle in hand*). I will curse her hotter than the oldest cinder in hell. But pray, begrudge me not my anger!

Elizabeth. Your anger! I only ask you—

Proctor. Woman, am I so base? Do you truly think me base?

Elizabeth. I never called you base.

Proctor. Then how do you charge me with such a promise? The promise that a stallion gives a mare I gave that girl!

Elizabeth. Then why do you anger with me when I bid you break it?

Proctor. Because it speaks deceit, and I am honest! But I'll plead no more! I see now your spirit twists around the single error of my life, and I will never tear it free!

Elizabeth (*crying out*). You'll tear it free—when you come to know that I will be your only wife, or no wife at all! She has an arrow in you yet, John Proctor, and you know it well!

(*Quite suddenly, as though from the air, a figure appears in the doorway. They start slightly. It is* Mr. Hale. *He is different now—drawn a little, and there is a quality of deference, even of guilt, about his manner now.*)

Hale. Good evening.

Proctor (*still in his shock*). Why, Mr. Hale! Good evening to you, sir. Come in, come in.

Hale (*to* Elizabeth). I hope I do not startle you.

Elizabeth. No, no, it's only that I heard no horse—

Hale. You are Goodwife Proctor.

Proctor. Aye; Elizabeth.

Hale (*nods, then*). I hope you're not off to bed yet.

Proctor (*setting down his gun*). No, no. (Hale *comes further into the room. And* Proctor, *to explain his nervousness*) We are not used to visitors after dark, but you're welcome here. Will you sit you down, sir?

Hale. I will. He sits. Let you sit, Goodwife Proctor.

(*She does, never letting him out of her sight. There is a pause as* Hale *looks about the room.*)

Proctor (*to break the silence*). Will you drink cider, Mr. Hale?

Hale. No, it rebels my stomach; I have some further traveling yet tonight. Sit you down, sir. (Proctor *sits.*) I will not keep you long, but I have some business with you.

Proctor. Business of the court?

Hale. No—no, I come of my own, without the court's authority. Hear me. (*He wets his lips.*) I know not if you are aware, but your wife's name is— mentioned in the court.

Proctor. We know it, sir. Our Mary Warren told us. We are entirely amazed.

Hale. I am a stranger here, as you know. And in my ignorance I find it hard to draw a clear opinion of them that come accused before the court. And so this afternoon, and now tonight, I go from house to house—I come now from Rebecca Nurse's house and—

Elizabeth (*shocked*). Rebecca's charged!

Hale. God forbid such a one be charged. She is, however—mentioned somewhat.

Elizabeth (*with an attempt at a laugh*). You will never believe, I hope, that Rebecca trafficked with the Devil.

Hale. Woman, it is possible.

Proctor (*taken aback*). Surely you cannot think so.

Hale. This is a strange time, Mister. No man may longer doubt the powers of the dark are gathered in monstrous attack upon this village. There is too much evidence now to deny it. You will agree, sir?

Proctor (*evading*). I—have no knowledge in that line. But it's hard to think so pious a woman be secretly a Devil's bitch after seventy year of such good prayer.

Hale. Aye. But the Devil is a wily one, you cannot deny it. However, she is far from accused, and I know she will not be. (*Pause.*) I thought, sir, to put some questions as to the Christian character of this house, if you'll permit me.

Proctor (*coldly, resentful*). Why, we—have no fear of questions, sir.

Hale. Good, then. (*He makes himself more comfortable.*) In the book of record that Mr. Parris keeps, I note that you are rarely in the church on Sabbath Day.

Proctor. No, sir, you are mistaken.

Hale. Twenty-six time in seventeen month, sir. I must call that rare. Will you tell me why you are so absent?

Proctor. Mr. Hale, I never knew I must account to that man for I come to church or stay at home. My wife were sick this winter.

Hale. So I am told. But you, Mister, why could you not come alone?

Proctor. I surely did come when I could, and when I could not I prayed in this house.

Hale. Mr. Proctor, your house is not a church; your theology must tell you that.

Proctor. It does, sir, it does; and it tells me that a minister may pray to God without he have golden candlesticks upon the altar.

Hale. What golden candlesticks?

Proctor. Since we built the church there were pewter candlesticks upon the altar; Francis Nurse made them, y'know, and a sweeter hand never touched the metal. But Parris came, and for twenty week he preach nothin' but golden candlesticks until he had them. I labor the earth from dawn of day to blink of night, and I tell you true, when I look to heaven and see my money glaring at his elbows— it hurt my prayer, sir, it hurt my prayer. I think, sometimes, the man dreams cathedrals, not clapboard meetin' houses.

Hale (*thinks, then*). And yet, Mister, a Christian on Sabbath Day must be in church. (*Pause.*) Tell me— you have three children?

Proctor. Aye. Boys.

Hale. How comes it that only two are baptized?

Proctor (*starts to speak, then stops, then, as though unable to restrain this*). I like it not that Mr. Parris should lay his hand upon my baby. I see no light of God in that man. I'll not conceal it.

Hale. I must say it, Mr. Proctor; that is not for you to decide. The man's ordained, therefore the light of God is in him.

Proctor (*flushed with resentment but trying to smile*). What's your suspicion, Mr. Hale?

Hale. No, no, I have no—

Proctor. I nailed the roof upon the church, I hung the door—

Hale. Oh, did you! That's a good sign, then.

Proctor. It may be I have been too quick to bring the man to book, but you cannot think we ever desired the destruction of religion. I think that's in your mind, is it not?

Hale (*not altogether giving way*). I—have—there is a softness in your record, sir, a softness.

Elizabeth. I think, maybe, we have been too hard with Mr. Parris. I think so. But sure we never loved the Devil here.

Hale (*nods, deliberating this. Then, with the voice of one administering a secret test*). Do you know your Commandments, Elizabeth?

Elizabeth (*without hesitation, even eagerly*). I surely do. There be no mark of blame upon my life, Mr. Hale. I am a convenanted Christian woman.

Hale. And you, Mister?

Proctor (*a trifle unsteadily*). I—am sure I do, sir.

Hale (*glances at her open face, then at John, then*). Let you repeat them, if you will.

Proctor. The Commandments.

Hale. Aye.

Proctor (*looking off, beginning to sweat*). Thou shalt not kill.

Hale. Aye.

Proctor (*counting on his fingers*). Thou shalt not steal. Thou shalt not covet thy neighbor's goods, nor make unto thee any graven image. Thou shalt not take the name of the Lord in vain; thou shalt have no other gods before me. (*With some hesitation.*)

Thou shalt remember the Sabbath Day and keep it holy. (*Pause. Then.*) Thou shalt honor thy father and mother. Thou shalt not bear false witness. (*He is stuck. He counts back on his fingers, knowing one is missing.*) Thou shalt not make unto thee any graven image.

Hale. You have said that twice, sir.

Proctor (*lost*). Aye. (*He is flailing for it.*)

Elizabeth (*delicately*). Adultery, John.

Proctor (*as though a secret arrow had pained his heart*). Aye. (*Trying to grin it away—to* Hale) You see, sir, between the two of us we do know them all. (Hale *only looks at* Proctor, *deep in his attempt to define this man.* Proctor *grows more uneasy.*) I think it be a small fault.

Hale. Theology, sir, is a fortress; no crack in a fortress may be accounted small. (*He rises; he seems worried now. He paces a little, in deep thought.*)

Proctor. There be no love for Satan in this house, Mister.

Hale. I pray it, I pray it dearly. (*He looks to both of them, an attempt at a smile on his face, but his misgivings are clear.*) Well, then—I'll bid you good night.

Elizabeth (*unable to restrain herself*). Mr. Hale. (*He turns.*) I do think you are suspecting me somewhat? Are you not?

Hale (*obviously disturbed—and evasive*). Goody Proctor, I do not judge you. My duty is to add what I may to the godly wisdom of the court. I pray you both good health and good fortune. (*To* John) Good night, sir. (*He starts out.*)

Elizabeth (*with a note of desperation*). I think you must tell him, John.

Hale. What's that?

Elizabeth (*restraining a call*). Will you tell him?

(*Slight pause.* Hale *looks questioningly at* John.)

Proctor (*with difficulty*). I—I have no witness and cannot prove it, except my word be taken. But I know the children's sickness had naught to do with witchcraft.

Hale (*stopped, struck*). Naught to do—?

Proctor. Mr. Parris discovered them sportin' in the woods. They were startled and took sick.

(*Pause.*)

Hale. Who told you this?

Proctor (*hesitates, then*). Abigail Williams.

Hale. Abigail!

Proctor. Aye.

Hale (*his eyes wide*). Abigail Williams told you it had naught to do with witchcraft!

Proctor. She told me the day you came, sir.

Hale (*suspiciously*). Why—why did you keep this?

Proctor. I never knew until tonight that the world is gone daft with this nonsense.

Hale. Nonsense! Mister, I have myself examined Tituba, Sarah Good, and numerous others that have confessed to dealing with the Devil. They have confessed it.

Proctor. And why not, if they must hang for denyin' it? There are them that will swear to anything before they'll hang; have you never thought of that?

Hale. I have. I—I have indeed. (*It is his own suspicion, but he resists it. He glances at* Elizabeth, *then at* John.) And you—would you testify to this in court?

Proctor. I—had not reckoned with goin' into court. But if I must I will.

Hale. Do you falter here?

Proctor. I falter nothing, but I may wonder if my story will be credited in such a court. I do wonder on it, when such a steady-minded minister as you will suspicion such a woman that never lied, and cannot, and the world knows she cannot! I may falter somewhat, Mister; I am no fool.

Hale (*quietly—it has impressed him*). Proctor, let you open with me now, for I have a rumor that troubles me. It's said you hold no belief that there may even be witches in the world. Is that true, sir?

Proctor (*he knows this is critical, and is striving against his disgust with* Hale *and with himself for even answering*). I know not what I have said, I may have said it. I have wondered if there be witches in the world—although I cannot believe they come among us now.

Hale. Then you do not believe—

Proctor. I have no knowledge of it; the Bible speaks of witches, and I will not deny them.

Hale. And you, woman?

Elizabeth. I—I cannot believe it.

Hale (*shocked*). You cannot!

Proctor. Elizabeth, you bewilder him!

Elizabeth (*to* Hale). I cannot think the Devil may own a woman's soul, Mr. Hale, when she keeps an upright way, as I have. I am a good woman, I know it; and if you believe I may do only good work in the world, and yet be secretly bound to Satan, then I must tell you, sir, I do not believe it.

Hale. But, woman, you do believe there are witches in—

Elizabeth. If you think that I am one, then I say there are none.

Hale. You surely do not fly against the Gospel, the Gospel—

Proctor. She believe in the Gospel, every word!

Elizabeth. Question Abigail Williams about the Gospel, not myself!

(Hale *stares at her.*)

Proctor. She do not mean to doubt the Gospel, sir, you cannot think it. This be a Christian house, sir, a Christian house.

Hale. God keep you both; let the third child be quickly baptized, and go you without fail each Sunday in to Sabbath prayer; and keep a solemn, quiet way among you. I think—

(Giles Corey *appears in doorway.*)

Giles. John!

Proctor. Giles! What's the matter?

Giles. They take my wife.

(Francis Nurse *enters.*)

Giles. And his Rebecca!

Proctor (*to* Francis). Rebecca's in the jail!

Francis. Aye, Cheever come and take her in his wagon. We've only now come from the jail, and they'll not even let us in to see them.

Elizabeth. They've surely gone wild now, Mr. Hale!

Francis (*going to* Hale). Reverend Hale! Can you not speak to the Deputy Governor? I'm sure he mistakes these people—

Hale. Pray calm yourself, Mr. Nurse.

Francis. My wife is the very brick and mortar of the church, Mr. Hale—(*indicating* Giles)—and Martha Corey, there cannot be a woman closer yet to God than Martha.

Hale. How is Rebecca charged, Mr. Nurse?

Francis (*with a mocking, half-hearted laugh*). For murder, she's charged! (*Mockingly quoting the warrant*) "For the marvelous and supernatural murder of Goody Putnam's babies." What am I to do, Mr. Hale?

Hale (*turns from* Francis, *deeply troubled, then*). Believe me, Mr. Nurse, if Rebecca Nurse be tainted, then nothing's left to stop the whole green world from burning. Let you rest upon the justice of the court; the court will send her home, I know it.

Francis. You cannot mean she will be tried in court!

Hale (*pleading*). Nurse, though our hearts break, we cannot flinch; these are new times, sir. There is a misty plot afoot so subtle we should be criminal to cling to old respects and ancient friendships. I have seen too many frightful proofs in court—the Devil is alive in Salem, and we dare not quail to follow wherever the accusing finger points!

Proctor (*angered*). How may such a woman murder children?

Hale (*in great pain*). Man, remember, until an hour before the Devil fell, God thought him beautiful in Heaven.

Giles. I never said my wife were a witch, Mr. Hale; I only said she were reading books!

Hale. Mr. Corey, exactly what complaint were made on your wife?

Giles. That bloody mongrel Walcott charge her. Y'see, he buy a pig of my wife four or five year ago, and the pig died soon after. So he come dancin' in for his money back. So my Martha, she says to him, "Walcott, if you haven't the wit to feed a pig properly, you'll not live to own many," she says. Now he goes to court and claims that from that day to this he cannot keep a pig alive for more than four weeks because my Martha bewitch them with her books!

(*Enter* Ezekiel Cheever. *A shocked silence.*)

Cheever. Good evening to you, Proctor.

Proctor. Why, Mr. Cheever. Good evening.

Cheever. Good evening, all. Good evening, Mr. Hale.

Proctor. I hope you come not on business of the court.

Cheever. I do, Proctor, aye. I am clerk of the court now, y'know.

(*Enter* Marshal Herrick, *a man in his early thirties, who is somewhat shamefaced at the moment.*)

Giles. It's a pity, Ezekiel, that an honest tailor might have gone to Heaven must burn in Hell. You'll burn for this, do you know it?

Cheever. You know yourself I must do as I'm told. You surely know that, Giles. And I'd as lief you'd not be sending me to Hell. I like not the sound of it, I tell you; I like not the sound of it. (*He fears* Proctor, *but starts to reach inside his coat.*) Now believe me, Proctor, how heavy be the law, all its tonnage I do carry on my back tonight. (*He takes out a warrant.*) I have a warrant for your wife.

Proctor (*to* Hale). You said she were not charged!

Hale. I know nothin' of it. (*To* Cheever) When were she charged?

Cheever. I am given sixteen warrant tonight, sir, and she is one.

Proctor. Who charged her?

Cheever. Why, Abigail Williams charge her.

Proctor. On what proof, what proof?

Cheever (*looking about the room*). Mr. Proctor, I have little time. The court bid me search your house, but I like not to search a house. So will you hand me any poppets that your wife may keep here?

Proctor. Poppets?

Elizabeth. I never kept no poppets, not since I were a girl.

Cheever (*embarrassed, glancing toward the mantel where sits* Mary Warren's *poppet*). I spy a poppet, Goody Proctor.

Elizabeth. Oh! Going for it: Why, this is Mary's.

Cheever (*shyly*). Would you please to give it to me?

Elizabeth (*handing it to him, asks* Hale). Has the court discovered a text in poppets now?

Cheever (*carefully holding the poppet*). Do you keep any others in this house?

Proctor. No, nor this one either till tonight. What signifies a poppet?

Cheever. Why, a poppet—(*he gingerly turns the poppet over*)—a poppet may signify—Now, woman, will you please to come with me?

Proctor. She will not! (*To* Elizabeth) Fetch Mary here.

Cheever (*ineptly reaching toward* Elizabeth). No, no, I am forbid to leave her from my sight.

Proctor (*pushing his arm away*). You'll leave her out of sight and out of mind, Mister. Fetch Mary, Elizabeth. (Elizabeth *goes upstairs.*)

Hale. What signifies a poppet, Mr. Cheever?

Cheever (*turning the poppet over in his hands*). Why, they say it may signify that she—(*He has lifted the poppet's skirt, and his eyes widen in astonished fear.*) Why, this, this—

Proctor (*reaching for the poppet*). What's there?

Cheever. Why—(*He draws out a long needle from the poppet*)—it is a needle! Herrick, Herrick, it is a needle!

(Herrick *comes toward him.*)

Proctor (*angrily, bewildered*). And what signifies a needle!

Cheever (*his hands shaking*). Why, this go hard with her, Proctor, this—I had my doubts, Proctor, I had my doubts, but here's calamity. (*To* Hale, *showing the needle*) You see it, sir, it is a needle!

Hale. Why? What meanin' has it?

Cheever (*wide-eyed, trembling*). The girl, the Williams girl, Abigail Williams, sir. She sat to dinner in Reverend Parris's house tonight, and without word nor warnin' she falls to the floor. Like a struck beast, he says, and screamed a scream that a bull would weep to hear. And he goes to save her, and, stuck two inches in the flesh of her belly, he draw a needle out. And demandin' of her how she come to be so stabbed, she—(*to* Proctor *now*)—testify it were your wife's familiar spirit pushed it in.

Proctor. Why, she done it herself! (*To* Hale) I hope you're not takin' this for proof, Mister!

(Hale, *struck by the proof, is silent.*)

Cheever. 'Tis hard proof! (*To* Hale) I find here a poppet Goody Proctor keeps. I have found it, sir. And in the belly of the poppet a needle's stuck. I tell you true, Proctor, I never warranted to see such proof of Hell, and I bid you obstruct me not, for I—

(*Enter* Elizabeth *with* Mary Warren. Proctor, *seeing* Mary Warren, *draws her by the arm to* Hale.)

Proctor. Here now! Mary, how did this poppet come into my house?

Mary Warren (*frightened for herself, her voice very small*). What poppet's that, sir?

Proctor (*impatiently, pointing at the doll in* Cheever's *hand*). This poppet, this poppet.

Mary Warren (*evasively, looking at it*). Why, I—I think it is mine.

Proctor. It is your poppet, is it not?

Mary Warren (*not understanding the direction of this*). It— is, sir.

Proctor. And how did it come into this house?

Mary Warren (*glancing about at the avid faces*). Why—I made it in the court, sir, and—give it to Goody Proctor tonight.

Proctor (*to* Hale). Now, sir—do you have it?

Hale. Mary Warren, a needle have been found inside this poppet.

Mary Warren (*bewildered*). Why, I meant no harm by it, sir.

Proctor (*quickly*). You stuck that needle in yourself?

Mary Warren. I—I believe I did, sir, I—

Proctor (*to* Hale). What say you now?

Hale (*watching* Mary Warren *closely*). Child, you are certain this be your natural memory? May it be, perhaps, that someone conjures you even now to say this?

Mary Warren. Conjures me? Why, no, sir, I am entirely myself, I think. Let you ask Susanna Walcott—she saw me sewin' it in court. Or better still: Ask Abby, Abby sat beside me when I made it.

Proctor (*to* Hale, *of* Cheever). Bid him begone. Your mind is surely settled now. Bid him out, Mr. Hale.

Elizabeth. What signifies a needle?

Hale. Mary—you charge a cold and cruel murder on Abigail.

Mary Warren. Murder! I charge no—

Hale. Abigail were stabbed tonight; a needle were found stuck into her belly—

Elizabeth. And she charges me?

Hale. Aye.

Elizabeth (*her breath knocked out*). Why—! The girl is murder! She must be ripped out of the world!

Cheever (*pointing at* Elizabeth). You've heard that, sir! Ripped out of the world! Herrick, you heard it!

Proctor (*suddenly snatching the warrant out of* Cheever's *hands*). Out with you.

Cheever. Proctor, you dare not touch the warrant.

Proctor (*ripping the warrant*). Out with you!

Cheever. You've ripped the Deputy Governor's warrant, man!

Proctor. Damn the Deputy Governor! Out of my house!

Hale. Now, Proctor, Proctor!

Proctor. Get y'gone with them! You are a broken minister.

Hale. Proctor, if she is innocent, the court—

Proctor. If she is innocent! Why do you never wonder if Parris be innocent, or Abigail? Is the accuser always holy now? Were they born this morning as clean as God's fingers? I'll tell you what's walking Salem—vengeance is walking Salem. We are what we always were in Salem, but now the little crazy children are jangling the keys of the kingdom, and common vengeance writes the law! This warrant's vengeance! I'll not give my wife to vengeance!

Elizabeth. I'll go, John—

Proctor. You will not go!

Herrick. I have nine men outside. You cannot keep her. The law binds me, John, I cannot budge.

Proctor (*to* Hale, *ready to break him*). Will you see her taken?

Hale. Proctor, the court is just—

Proctor. Pontius Pilate! God will not let you wash your hands of this!

Elizabeth. John—I think I must go with them. (*He cannot bear to look at her.*) Mary, there is bread enough for the morning; you will bake, in the afternoon. Help Mr. Proctor as you were his daughter—you owe me that, and much more. (*She is fighting her weeping. To* Proctor) When the children wake, speak nothing of witchcraft—it will frighten them. (*She cannot go on.*)

Proctor. I will bring you home. I will bring you soon.

Elizabeth. Oh, John, bring me soon!

Proctor. I will fall like an ocean on that court! Fear nothing, Elizabeth.

Elizabeth (*with great fear*). I will fear nothing. (*She looks about the room, as though to fix it in her mind.*) Tell the children I have gone to visit someone sick.

(*She walks out the door,* Herrick *and* Cheever *behind her. For a moment,* Proctor *watches from the doorway. The clank of chain is heard.*)

Proctor. Herrick! Herrick, don't chain her! (*He rushes out the door. From outside*) Damn you, man, you will not chain her! Off with them! I'll not have it! I will not have her chained!

(*There are other men's voices against his.* Hale, *in a fever of guilt and uncertainty, turns from the door to avoid the sight;* Mary Warren *bursts into tears and sits weeping.* Giles Corey *calls to* Hale.)

Giles. And yet silent, minister? It is fraud, you know it is fraud! What keeps you, man?

(Proctor *is half braced, half pushed into the room by two deputies and* Herrick.)

Proctor. I'll pay you, Herrick, I will surely pay you!

Herrick (*panting*). In God's name, John, I cannot help myself. I must chain them all. Now let you keep inside this house till I am gone! (*He goes out with his deputies.*)

(Proctor *stands there, gulping air. Horses and a wagon creaking are heard.*)

Hale (*in great uncertainty*). Mr. Proctor—

Proctor. Out of my sight!

Hale. Charity, Proctor, charity. What I have heard in her favor, I will not fear to testify in court. God help me, I cannot judge her guilty or innocent—I know not. Only this consider: the world goes mad, and it profit nothing you should lay the cause to the vengeance of a little girl.

Proctor. You are a coward! Though you be ordained in God's own tears, you are a coward now!

Hale. Proctor, I cannot think God be provoked so grandly by such a petty cause. The jails are packed—our greatest judges sit in Salem now—and hangin's promised. Man, we must look to cause proportionate. Were there murder done, perhaps, and never brought to light? Abomination? Some secret blasphemy that stinks to Heaven? Think on cause, man, and let you help me to discover it. For there's your way, believe it, there is your only way, when such confusion strikes upon the world. (*He goes to* Giles *and* Francis.) Let you counsel among yourselves; think on your village and what may have drawn from heaven such thundering wrath upon you all. I shall pray God open up our eyes.

(Hale *goes out.*)

Francis (*struck by* Hale's *mood*). I never heard no murder done in Salem.

Proctor (*he has been reached by* Hale's *words*). Leave me, Francis, leave me.

Giles (*shaken*). John—tell me, are we lost?

Proctor. Go home now, Giles. We'll speak on it tomorrow.

Giles. Let you think on it. We'll come early, eh?

Proctor. Aye. Go now, Giles.

Giles. Good night, then.

(Giles Corey *goes out. After a moment*)

Mary Warren (*in a fearful squeak of a voice*). Mr. Proctor, very likely they'll let her come home once they're given proper evidence.

Proctor. You're coming to the court with me, Mary. You will tell it in the court.

Mary Warren. I cannot charge murder on Abigail.

Proctor (*moving menacingly toward her*). You will tell the court how that poppet come here and who stuck the needle in.

Mary Warren. She'll kill me for sayin' that! (Proctor *continues toward her.*) Abby'll charge lechery on you, Mr. Proctor!

Proctor (*halting*). She's told you!

Mary Warren. I have known it, sir. She'll ruin you with it, I know she will.

Proctor (*hesitating, and with deep hatred of himself*). Good. Then her saintliness is done with. (*Mary backs from him.*) We will slide together into our pit; you will tell the court what you know.

Mary Warren (*in terror*). I cannot, they'll turn on me—

(*Proctor strides and catches her, and she is repeating, "I cannot, I cannot!"*)

Proctor. My wife will never die for me! I will bring your guts into your mouth but that goodness will not die for me!

Mary Warren (*struggling to escape him*). I cannot do it, I cannot!

Proctor (*grasping her by the throat as though he would strangle her*). Make your peace with it! Now Hell and Heaven grapple on our backs, and all our old pretense is ripped away—make your peace! (*He throws her to the floor, where she sobs, "I cannot, I cannot . . ." And now, half to himself, staring, and turning to the open door*) Peace. It is a providence, and no great change; we are only what we always were, but naked now. (*He walks as though toward a great horror, facing the open sky.*) Aye, naked! And the wind, God's icy wind, will blow!

(*And she is over and over again sobbing, "I cannot, I cannot, I cannot," as*)

THE CURTAIN FALLS*

---

* Act II, Scene 2, which appeared in the original production, was dropped by the author from the published reading

version, the *Collected Plays,* and all Compass editions prior to 1971. It has not been included in most productions subsequent to the revival at New York's Martinique Theatre in 1958 and was dropped by Sir Laurence Olivier in his London production in 1965. It is included here as an appendix on page 154.

Act Three

....

(*The vestry room of the Salem meeting house, now serving as the anteroom of the General Court.*)

(*As the curtain rises, the room is empty, but for sunlight pouring through two high windows in the back wall. The room is solemn, even forbidding. Heavy beams jut out, boards of random widths make up the walls. At the right are two doors leading into the meeting house proper, where the court is being held. At the left another door leads outside.*)

(*There is a plain bench at the left, and another at the right. In the center a rather long meeting table, with stools and a considerable armchair snugged up to it.*)

(*Through the partitioning wall at the right we hear a prosecutor's voice,* Judge Hathorne's, *asking a question; then a woman's voice,* Martha Corey's, *replying.*)

Hathorne's Voice. Now, Martha Corey, there is abundant evidence in our hands to show that you have given yourself to the reading of fortunes. Do you deny it?

Martha Corey's Voice. I am innocent to a witch. I know not what a witch is.

Hathorne's Voice. How do you know, then, that you are not a witch?

Martha Corey's Voice. If I were, I would know it.

Hathorne's Voice. Why do you hurt these children?

Martha Corey's Voice. I do not hurt them. I scorn it!

Giles' Voice (*roaring*). I have evidence for the court!

(*Voices of townspeople rise in excitement.*)

Danforth's Voice. You will keep your seat!

Giles' Voice. Thomas Putnam is reaching out for land!

Danforth's Voice. Remove that man, Marshal!

Giles' Voice. You're hearing lies, lies!

(*A roaring goes up from the people.*)

Hathorne's Voice. Arrest him, excellency!

Giles' Voice. I have evidence. Why will you not hear my evidence?

(*The door opens and* Giles *is half carried into the vestry room by* Herrick.)

Giles. Hands off, damn you, let me go!

Herrick. Giles, Giles!

Giles. Out of my way, Herrick! I bring evidence—

Herrick. You cannot go in there, Giles; it's a court!

(*Enter* Hale *from the court.*)

Hale. Pray be calm a moment.

Giles. You, Mr. Hale, go in there and demand I speak.

Hale. A moment, sir, a moment.

Giles. They'll be hangin' my wife!

(Judge Hathorne *enters. He is in his sixties, a bitter, remorseless Salem judge.*)

Hathorne. How do you dare come roarin' into this court! Are you gone daft, Corey?

Giles. You're not a Boston judge yet, Hathorne. You'll not call me daft!

(*Enter* Deputy Governor Danforth *and, behind him,* Ezekiel Cheever *and* Parris. *On his appearance, silence falls.* Danforth *is a grave man in his sixties, of some humor and sophistication that does not, however, interfere with an exact loyalty to his position and his cause. He comes down to* Giles, *who awaits his wrath.*)

Danforth (*looking directly at* Giles). Who is this man?

Parris. Giles Corey, sir, and a more contentious—

Giles (*to* Parris). I am asked the question, and I am old enough to answer it! (*To* Danforth, *who impresses him and to whom he smiles through his strain*) My name is Corey, sir, Giles Corey. I have six hundred acres, and timber in addition. It is my wife you be condemning now. (*He indicates the courtroom.*)

Danforth. And how do you imagine to help her cause with such contemptuous riot? Now be gone. Your old age alone keeps you out of jail for this.

Giles (*beginning to plead*). They be tellin' lies about my wife, sir, I—

Danforth. Do you take it upon yourself to determine what this court shall believe and what it shall set aside?

Giles. Your Excellency, we mean no disrespect for—

Danforth. Disrespect indeed! It is disruption, Mister. This is the highest court of the supreme government of this province, do you know it?

Giles (*beginning to weep*). Your Excellency, I only said she were readin' books, sir, and they come and take her out of my house for—

Danforth (*mystified*). Books! What books?

Giles (*through helpless sobs*). It is my third wife, sir; I never had no wife that be so taken with books, and I thought to find the cause of it, d'y'see, but it were no witch I blamed her for. (*He is openly weeping.*) I have broke charity with the woman, I have broke charity with her. (*He covers his face, ashamed.* Danforth *is respectfully silent.*)

Hale. Excellency, he claims hard evidence for his wife's defense. I think that in all justice you must—

Danforth. Then let him submit his evidence in proper affidavit. You are certainly aware of our procedure here, Mr. Hale. (*To* Herrick) Clear this room.

Herrick. Come now, Giles. (*He gently pushes* Corey *out.*)

Francis. We are desperate, sir; we come here three days now and cannot be heard.

Danforth. Who is this man?

Francis. Francis Nurse, Your Excellency.

Hale. His wife's Rebecca that were condemned this morning.

Danforth. Indeed! I am amazed to find you in such uproar. I have only good report of your character, Mr. Nurse.

Hathorne. I think they must both be arrested in contempt, sir.

Danforth (*to* Francis). Let you write your plea, and in due time I will—

Francis. Excellency, we have proof for your eyes; God forbid you shut them to it. The girls, sir, the girls are frauds.

Danforth. What's that?

Francis. We have proof of it, sir. They are all deceiving you.

(Danforth *is shocked, but studying* Francis.)

Hathorne. This is contempt, sir, contempt!

Danforth. Peace, Judge Hathorne. Do you know who I am, Mr. Nurse?

Francis. I surely do, sir, and I think you must be a wise judge to be what you are.

Danforth. And do you know that near to four hundred are in the jails from Marblehead to Lynn, and upon my signature?

Francis. I—

Danforth. And seventy-two condemned to hang by that signature?

Francis. Excellency, I never thought to say it to such a weighty judge, but you are deceived.

(*Enter* Giles Corey *from left. All turn to see as he beckons in* Mary Warren *with* Proctor. Mary *is keeping her eyes to the ground;* Proctor *has her elbow as though she were near collapse.*)

Parris (*on seeing her, in shock*). Mary Warren! (*He goes directly to bend close to her face.*) What are you about here?

Proctor (*pressing* Parris *away from her with a gentle but firm motion of protectiveness*). She would speak with the Deputy Governor.

Danforth (*shocked by this, turns to* Herrick). Did you not tell me Mary Warren were sick in bed?

Herrick. She were, Your Honor. When I go to fetch her to the court last week, she said she were sick.

Giles. She has been strivin' with her soul all week, Your Honor; she comes now to tell the truth of this to you.

Danforth. Who is this?

Proctor. John Proctor, sir. Elizabeth Proctor is my wife.

Parris. Beware this man, Your Excellency, this man is mischief.

Hale (*excitedly*). I think you must hear the girl, sir, she—

Danforth (*who has become very interested in* Mary Warren *and only raises a hand toward* Hale). Peace. What would you tell us, Mary Warren?

(Proctor *looks at her, but she cannot speak.*)

Proctor. She never saw no spirits, sir.

Danforth (*with great alarm and surprise, to* Mary). Never saw no spirits!

Giles (*eagerly*). Never.

Proctor (*reaching into his jacket*). She has signed a deposition, sir—

Danforth (*instantly*). No, no, I accept no depositions. (*He is rapidly calculating this; he turns from her to* Proctor.) Tell me, Mr. Proctor, have you given out this story in the village?

Proctor. We have not.

Parris. They've come to overthrow the court, sir! This man is—

Danforth. I pray you, Mr. Parris. Do you know, Mr. Proctor, that the entire contention of the state in these trials is that the voice of Heaven is speaking through the children?

Proctor. I know that, sir.

Danforth (*thinks, staring at* Proctor, *then turns to* Mary Warren). And you, Mary Warren, how came you to cry out people for sending their spirits against you?

Mary Warren. It were pretense, sir.

Danforth. I cannot hear you.

Proctor. It were pretense, she says.

Danforth. Ah? And the other girls? Susanna Walcott, and—the others? They are also pretending?

Mary Warren. Aye, sir.

Danforth (*wide-eyed*). Indeed. (*Pause. He is baffled by this. He turns to study* Proctor's *face.*)

Parris (*in a sweat*). Excellency, you surely cannot think to let so vile a lie be spread in open court!

Danforth. Indeed not, but it strike hard upon me that she will dare come here with such a tale. Now, Mr. Proctor, before I decide whether I shall hear you or not, it is my duty to tell you this. We burn a hot fire here; it melts down all concealment.

Proctor. I know that, sir.

Danforth. Let me continue. I understand well, a husband's tenderness may drive him to extravagance in defense of a wife. Are you certain in your conscience, Mister, that your evidence is the truth?

Proctor. It is. And you will surely know it.

Danforth. And you thought to declare this revelation in the open court before the public?

Proctor. I thought I would, aye—with your permission.

Danforth (*his eyes narrowing*). Now, sir, what is your purpose in so doing?

Proctor. Why, I—I would free my wife, sir.

Danforth. There lurks nowhere in your heart, nor hidden in your spirit, any desire to undermine this court?

Proctor (*with the faintest faltering*). Why, no, sir.

Cheever (*clears his throat, awakening*). I—Your Excellency.

Danforth. Mr. Cheever.

Cheever. I think it be my duty, sir—(*Kindly, to* Proctor) You'll not deny it, John. (*To* Danforth) When we come to take his wife, he damned the court and ripped your warrant.

Parris. Now you have it!

Danforth. He did that, Mr. Hale?

Hale (*takes a breath*). Aye, he did.

Proctor. It were a temper, sir. I knew not what I did.

Danforth (*studying him*). Mr. Proctor.

Proctor. Aye, sir.

Danforth (*straight into his eyes*). Have you ever seen the Devil?

Proctor. No, sir.

Danforth. You are in all respects a Gospel Christian?

Proctor. I am, sir.

Parris. Such a Christian that will not come to church but once in a month!

Danforth (*restrained—he is curious*). Not come to church?

Proctor. I—I have no love for Mr. Parris. It is no secret. But God I surely love.

Cheever. He plow on Sunday, sir.

Danforth. Plow on Sunday!

Cheever (*apologetically*). I think it be evidence, John. I am an official of the court, I cannot keep it.

Proctor. I—I have once or twice plowed on Sunday. I have three children, sir, and until last year my land give little.

Giles. You'll find other Christians that do plow on Sunday if the truth be known.

Hale. Your Honor, I cannot think you may judge the man on such evidence.

Danforth. I judge nothing. (*Pause. He keeps watching* Proctor, *who tries to meet his gaze.*) I tell you straight, Mister—I have seen marvels in this court. I have seen people choked before my eyes by spirits; I have seen them stuck by pins and slashed by daggers. I have until this moment not the slightest reason to suspect that the children may be deceiving me. Do you understand my meaning?

Proctor. Excellency, does it not strike upon you that so many of these women have lived so long with such upright reputation, and—

Parris. Do you read the Gospel, Mr. Proctor?

Proctor. I read the Gospel.

Parris. I think not, or you should surely know that Cain were an upright man, and yet he did kill Abel.

Proctor. Aye, God tells us that. (*To* Danforth.) But who tells us Rebecca Nurse murdered seven babies by sending out her spirit on them? It is the children only, and this one will swear she lied to you.

(Danforth *considers, then beckons* Hathorne *to him.* Hathorne *leans in, and he speaks in his ear.* Hathorne *nods.*)

Hathorne. Aye, she's the one.

Danforth. Mr. Proctor, this morning, your wife send me a claim in which she states that she is pregnant now.

Proctor. My wife pregnant!

Danforth. There be no sign of it—we have examined her body.

Proctor. But if she say she is pregnant, then she must be! That woman will never lie, Mr. Danforth.

Danforth. She will not?

Proctor. Never, sir, never.

Danforth. We have thought it too convenient to be credited. However, if I should tell you now that I will let her be kept another month; and if she begin to show her natural signs, you shall have her living yet another year until she is delivered—what say you to that? (John Proctor *is struck silent.*) Come now. You say your only purpose is to save your wife. Good, then, she is saved at least this year, and a year is long. What say you, sir? It is done now. (*In conflict,* Proctor *glances at* Francis *and* Giles.) Will you drop this charge?

Proctor. I—I think I cannot.

Danforth (*now an almost imperceptible hardness in his voice*). Then your purpose is somewhat larger.

Parris. He's come to overthrow this court, Your Honor!

Proctor. These are my friends. Their wives are also accused—

Danforth (*with a sudden briskness of manner*). I judge you not, sir. I am ready to hear your evidence.

Proctor. I come not to hurt the court; I only—

Danforth (*cutting him off*). Marshal, go into the court and bid Judge Stoughton and Judge Sewall declare recess for one hour. And let them go to the tavern, if they will. All witnesses and prisoners are to be kept in the building.

Herrick. Aye, sir. (*Very deferentially*) If I may say it, sir, I know this man all my life. It is a good man, sir.

Danforth (*it is the reflection on himself he resents*). I am sure of it, Marshal. (Herrick *nods, then goes out.*) Now, what deposition do you have for us, Mr. Proctor? And I beg you be clear, open as the sky, and honest.

Proctor (*as he takes out several papers*). I am no lawyer, so I'll—

Danforth. The pure in heart need no lawyers. Proceed as you will.

Proctor (*handing* Danforth *a paper*). Will you read this first, sir? It's a sort of testament. The people signing it declare their good opinion of Rebecca, and my wife, and Martha Corey. (Danforth *looks down at the paper.*)

Parris (*to enlist* Danforth's *sarcasm*). Their good opinion! (*But* Danforth *goes on reading, and* Proctor *is heartened.*)

Proctor. These are all landholding farmers, members of the church. (*Delicately, trying to point out a paragraph*). If you'll notice, sir—they've known the women many years and never saw no sign they had dealings with the Devil.

(Parris *nervously moves over and reads over* Danforth's *shoulder.*)

Danforth (*glancing down a long list*). How many names are here?

Francis. Ninety-one, Your Excellency.

Parris (*sweating*). These people should be summoned. (Danforth *looks up at him questioningly.*) For questioning.

Francis (*trembling with anger*). Mr. Danforth, I gave them all my word no harm would come to them for signing this.

Parris. This is a clear attack upon the court!

Hale (*to* Parris, *trying to contain himself*). Is every defense an attack upon the court? Can no one—?

Parris. All innocent and Christian people are happy for the courts in Salem! These people are gloomy for it. (*To* Danforth *directly*) And I think you will want to know, from each and every one of them, what discontents them with you!

Hathorne. I think they ought to be examined, sir.

Danforth. It is not necessarily an attack, I think. Yet—

Francis. These are all covenanted Christians, sir.

Danforth. Then I am sure they may have nothing to fear. (*Hands* Cheever *the paper.*) Mr. Cheever, have warrants drawn for all of these—arrest for examination. (*To* Proctor) Now, Mister, what other information do you have for us? (*Francis* is still *standing, horrified.*) You may sit, Mr. Nurse.

Francis. I have brought trouble on these people; I have—

Danforth. No, old man, you have not hurt these people if they are of good conscience. But you must understand, sir, that a person is either with this court or he must be counted against it, there be no road between. This is a sharp time, now, a precise time—we live no longer in the dusky afternoon when evil mixed itself with good and befuddled the world. Now, by God's grace, the shining sun is up, and them that fear not light will surely praise it. I hope you will be one of those. (Mary Warren *suddenly sobs.*) She's not hearty, I see.

Proctor. No, she's not, sir. (*To Mary, bending to her, holding her hand, quietly*) Now remember what the angel Raphael said to the boy Tobias. Remember it.

Mary Warren (*hardly audible*). Aye.

Proctor. "Do that which is good, and no harm shall come to thee."

Mary Warren. Aye.

Danforth. Come, man, we wait you.

(Marshal Herrick *returns, and takes his post at the door.*)

Giles. John, my deposition, give him mine.

Proctor. Aye. (*He hands* Danforth *another paper.*) This is Mr. Corey's deposition.

Danforth. Oh? (*He looks down at it. Now* Hathorne *comes behind him and reads with him.*)

Hathorne (*suspiciously*). What lawyer drew this, Corey?

Giles. You know I never hired a lawyer in my life, Hathorne.

Danforth (*finishing the reading*). It is very well phrased. My compliments. Mr. Parris, if Mr. Putnam is in the court, will you bring him in? (Hathorne *takes the deposition, and walks to the window with it.* Parris *goes into the court.*) You have no legal training, Mr. Corey?

Giles (*very pleased*). I have the best, sir—I am thirty-three time in court in my life. And always plaintiff, too.

Danforth. Oh, then you're much put-upon.

Giles. I am never put-upon; I know my rights, sir, and I will have them. You know, your father tried a case of mine—might be thirty-five year ago, I think.

Danforth. Indeed.

Giles. He never spoke to you of it?

Danforth. No, I cannot recall it.

Giles. That's strange, he give me nine pound damages. He were a fair judge, your father. Y'see, I had a white mare that time, and this fellow come to borrow the mare— (*Enter* Parris *with* Thomas Putnam. *When he sees* Putnam, *Giles' ease goes; he is hard.*) Aye, there he is.

Danforth. Mr. Putnam, I have here an accusation by Mr. Corey against you. He states that you coldly prompted your daughter to cry witchery upon George Jacobs that is now in jail.

Putnam. It is a lie.

Danforth (*turning to* Giles). Mr. Putnam states your charge is a lie. What say you to that?

Giles (*furious, his fists clenched*). A fart on Thomas Putnam, that is what I say to that!

Danforth. What proof do you submit for your charge, sir?

Giles. My proof is there! (*Pointing to the paper.*) If Jacobs hangs for a witch he forfeit up his property—that's law! And there is none but Putnam with the coin to buy so great a piece. This man is killing his neighbors for their land!

Danforth. But proof, sir, proof.

Giles (*pointing at his deposition*). The proof is there! I have it from an honest man who heard Putnam say it! The day his daughter cried out on Jacobs, he said she'd given him a fair gift of land.

Hathorne. And the name of this man?

Giles (*taken aback*). What name?

Hathorne. The man that give you this information.

Giles (*hesitates, then*). Why, I—I cannot give you his name.

Hathorne. And why not?

Giles (*hesitates, then bursts out*). You know well why not! He'll lay in jail if I give his name!

Hathorne. This is contempt of the court, Mr. Danforth!

Danforth (*to avoid that*). You will surely tell us the name.

Giles. I will not give you no name. I mentioned my wife's name once and I'll burn in hell long enough for that. I stand mute.

Danforth. In that case, I have no choice but to arrest you for contempt of this court, do you know that?

Giles. This is a hearing; you cannot clap me for contempt of a hearing.

Danforth. Oh, it is a proper lawyer! Do you wish me to declare the court in full session here? Or will you give me good reply?

Giles (*faltering*). I cannot give you no name, sir, I cannot.

Danforth. You are a foolish old man. Mr. Cheever, begin the record. The court is now in session. I ask you, Mr. Corey—

Proctor (*breaking in*). Your Honor—he has the story in confidence, sir, and he—

Parris. The Devil lives on such confidences! (*To Danforth*) Without confidences there could be no conspiracy, Your Honor!

Hathorne. I think it must be broken, sir.

Danforth (*to Giles*). Old man, if your informant tells the truth let him come here openly like a decent man. But if he hide in anonymity I must know why. Now sir, the government and central church demand of you the name of him who reported Mr. Thomas Putnam a common murderer.

Hale. Excellency—

Danforth. Mr. Hale.

Hale. We cannot blink it more. There is a prodigious fear of this court in the country—

Danforth. Then there is a prodigious guilt in the country. Are you afraid to be questioned here?

Hale. I may only fear the Lord, sir, but there is fear in the country nevertheless.

Danforth (*angered now*). Reproach me not with the fear in the country; there is fear in the country because there is a moving plot to topple Christ in the country!

Hale. But it does not follow that everyone accused is part of it.

Danforth. No uncorrupted man may fear this court, Mr. Hale! None! (*To* Giles.) You are under arrest in contempt of this court. Now sit you down and take counsel with yourself, or you will be set in the jail until you decide to answer all questions.

(Giles Corey *makes a rush for* Putnam. Proctor *lunges and holds him.*)

Proctor. No, Giles!

Giles (*over Proctor's shoulder at Putnam*). I'll cut your throat, Putnam, I'll kill you yet!

Proctor (*forcing him into a chair*). Peace, Giles, peace. (*Releasing him.*) We'll prove ourselves. Now we will. (*He starts to turn to Danforth.*)

Giles. Say nothin' more, John. (*Pointing at* Danforth.) He's only playin' you! He means to hang us all!

(*Mary Warren bursts into sobs.*)

Danforth. This is a court of law, Mister. I'll have no effrontery here!

Proctor. Forgive him, sir, for his old age. Peace, Giles, we'll prove it all now. (*He lifts up* Mary's *chin.*) You cannot weep, Mary. Remember the angel, what he say to the boy. Hold to it, now; there is your rock. (Mary *quiets. He takes out a paper, and turns to* Danforth.) This is Mary Warren's deposition. I—I would ask you remember, sir, while you read it, that until two week ago she were no different than the other children are today. (*He is speaking reasonably, restraining all his fears, his anger, his anxiety.*) You saw her scream, she howled, she swore familiar spirits choked her; she even testified that Satan, in the form of women now in jail, tried to win her soul away, and then when she refused—

Danforth. We know all this.

Proctor. Aye, sir. She swears now that she never saw Satan; nor any spirit, vague or clear, that Satan may have sent to hurt her. And she declares her friends are lying now.

(Proctor *starts to hand* Danforth *the deposition, and* Hale *comes up to* Danforth *in a trembling state.*)

Hale. Excellency, a moment. I think this goes to the heart of the matter.

Danforth (*with deep misgivings*). It surely does.

Hale. I cannot say he is an honest man; I know him little. But in all justice, sir, a claim so weighty cannot be argued by a farmer. In God's name, sir, stop here; send him home and let him come again with a lawyer—

Danforth (*patiently*). Now look you, Mr. Hale—

Hale. Excellency, I have signed seventy-two death warrants; I am a minister of the Lord, and I dare not take a life without there be a proof so immaculate no slightest qualm of conscience may doubt it.

Danforth. Mr. Hale, you surely do not doubt my justice.

Hale. I have this morning signed away the soul of Rebecca Nurse, Your Honor. I'll not conceal it, my hand shakes yet as with a wound! I pray you, sir, this argument let lawyers present to you.

Danforth. Mr. Hale, believe me; for a man of such terrible learning you are most bewildered—I hope you will forgive me. I have been thirty-two year at the bar, sir, and I should be confounded were I called upon to defend these people. Let you consider, now—(*To* Proctor *and the others.*) And I bid you all do likewise. In an ordinary crime, how does one defend the accused? One calls up witnesses to prove his innocence. But witchcraft is ipso facto, on its face and by its nature, an invisible crime, is it not? Therefore, who may possibly be witness to it? The witch and the victim. None other. Now we cannot hope the witch will accuse herself; granted? Therefore, we must rely upon her victims—and they do testify, the children certainly do testify. As for the witches, none will deny that we are most eager for all their confessions. Therefore, what is left for a lawyer to bring out? I think I have made my point. Have I not?

Hale. But this child claims the girls are not truthful, and if they are not—

Danforth. That is precisely what I am about to consider, sir. What more may you ask of me? Unless you doubt my probity?

Hale (*defeated*). I surely do not, sir. Let you consider it, then.

Danforth. And let you put your heart to rest. Her deposition, Mr. Proctor.

(Proctor *hands it to him.* Hathorne *rises, goes beside* Danforth, *and starts reading.* Parris *comes to his other side.* Danforth *looks at* John Proctor, *then proceeds to read.* Hale *gets up, finds position near the judge, reads too.* Proctor *glances at* Giles. Francis *prays silently, hands pressed together.* Cheever *waits placidly, the sublime official, dutiful.*

Mary Warren *sobs once.* John Proctor *touches her head reassuringly. Presently* Danforth *lifts his eyes, stands up, takes out a kerchief and blows his nose. The others stand aside as he moves in thought toward the window.*)

Parris (*hardly able to contain his anger and fear*). I should like to question—

Danforth (*his first real outburst, in which his contempt for* Parris *is clear*). Mr. Parris, I bid you be silent! (*He stands in silence, looking out the window. Now, having established that he will set the gait.*) Mr. Cheever, will you go into the court and bring the children here? (Cheever *gets up and goes out upstage.* Danforth *now turns to* Mary.) Mary Warren, how came you to this turnabout? Has Mr. Proctor threatened you for this deposition?

Mary Warren. No, sir.

Danforth. Has he ever threatened you?

Mary Warren (*weaker*). No, sir.

Danforth (*sensing a weakening*). Has he threatened you?

Mary Warren. No, sir.

Danforth. Then you tell me that you sat in my court, callously lying, when you knew that people would hang by your evidence? (*She does not answer.*) Answer me!

Mary Warren (*almost inaudibly*). I did, sir.

Danforth. How were you instructed in your life? Do you not know that God damns all liars? (*She cannot speak.*) Or is it now that you lie?

Mary Warren. No, sir—I am with God now.

Danforth. You are with God now.

Mary Warren. Aye, sir.

Danforth (*containing himself*). I will tell you this—you are either lying now, or you were lying in the court, and in either case you have committed perjury and you will go to jail for it. You cannot lightly say you lied, Mary. Do you know that?

Mary Warren. I cannot lie no more. I am with God, I am with God.

(*But she breaks into sobs at the thought of it, and the right door opens, and enter* Susanna Walcott, Mercy Lewis, Betty Parris, *and finally* Abigail. Cheever *comes to* Danforth.)

Cheever. Ruth Putnam's not in the court, sir, nor the other children.

Danforth. These will be sufficient. Sit you down, children. (*Silently they sit.*) Your friend, Mary Warren, has given us a deposition. In which she swears that she never saw familiar spirits, apparitions, nor any manifest of the Devil. She claims as well that none of you have seen these things either. (*Slight pause.*) Now, children, this is a court of law. The law, based upon the Bible, and the Bible, writ by Almighty God, forbid the practice of witchcraft, and describe death as the penalty thereof. But likewise, children, the law and Bible damn all bearers of false witness. (*Slight pause.*) Now then. It does not escape me that this deposition may be devised to blind us; it may well be that Mary Warren has been conquered by Satan, who sends her here to distract our sacred purpose. If so, her neck will break for it. But if she speak true, I bid you now drop your guile and confess your pretense, for a quick confession will go easier with you. (*Pause.*) Abigail Williams, rise. (Abigail *slowly rises.*) Is there any truth in this?

Abigail. No, sir.

Danforth (*thinks, glances at* Mary, *then back to* Abigail). Children, a very auger bit will now be turned into your souls until your honesty is proved. Will either of you change your positions now, or do you force me to hard questioning?

Abigail. I have naught to change, sir. She lies.

Danforth (*to* Mary). You would still go on with this?

Mary Warren (*faintly*). Aye, sir.

Danforth (*turning to* Abigail). A poppet were discovered in Mr. Proctor's house, stabbed by a needle. Mary Warren claims that you sat beside her in the court when she made it, and that you saw her make it and witnessed how she herself stuck her needle into it for safe-keeping. What say you to that?

Abigail (*with a slight note of indignation*). It is a lie, sir.

Danforth (*after a slight pause*). While you worked for Mr. Proctor, did you see poppets in that house?

Abigail. Goody Proctor always kept poppets.

Proctor. Your Honor, my wife never kept no poppets. Mary Warren confesses it was her poppet.

Cheever. Your Excellency.

Danforth. Mr. Cheever.

Cheever. When I spoke with Goody Proctor in that house, she said she never kept no poppets. But she said she did keep poppets when she were a girl.

Proctor. She has not been a girl these fifteen years, Your Honor.

Hathorne. But a poppet will keep fifteen years, will it not?

Proctor. It will keep if it is kept, but Mary Warren swears she never saw no poppets in my house, nor anyone else.

Parris. Why could there not have been poppets hid where no one ever saw them?

Proctor (*furious*). There might also be a dragon with five legs in my house, but no one has ever seen it.

Parris. We are here, Your Honor, precisely to discover what no one has ever seen.

Proctor. Mr. Danforth, what profit this girl to turn herself about? What may Mary Warren gain but hard questioning and worse?

Danforth. You are charging Abigail Williams with a marvelous cool plot to murder, do you understand that?

Proctor. I do, sir. I believe she means to murder.

Danforth (*pointing at* Abigail, *incredulously*). This child would murder your wife?

Proctor. It is not a child. Now hear me, sir. In the sight of the congregation she were twice this year put out of this meetin' house for laughter during prayer.

Danforth (*shocked, turning to* Abigail). What's this? Laughter during—!

Parris. Excellency, she were under Tituba's power at that time, but she is solemn now.

Giles. Aye, now she is solemn and goes to hang people!

Danforth. Quiet, man.

Hathorne. Surely it have no bearing on the question, sir. He charges contemplation of murder.

Danforth. Aye. (*He studies* Abigail *for a moment, then*) Continue, Mr. Proctor.

Proctor. Mary. Now tell the Governor how you danced in the woods.

Parris (*instantly*). Excellency, since I come to Salem this man is blackening my name. He—

Danforth. In a moment, sir. (*To* Mary Warren, *sternly, and surprised.*) What is this dancing?

Mary Warren. I—(*She glances at* Abigail, *who is staring down at her remorselessly. Then, appealing to* Proctor) Mr. Proctor—

Proctor (*taking it right up*). Abigail leads the girls to the woods, Your Honor, and they have danced there naked—

Parris. Your Honor, this—

Proctor (*at once*). Mr. Parris discovered them himself in the dead of night! There's the "child" she is!

Danforth (*it is growing into a nightmare, and he turns, astonished, to* Parris). Mr. Parris—

Parris. I can only say, sir, that I never found any of them naked, and this man is—

Danforth. But you discovered them dancing in the woods? (*Eyes on* Parris, *he points at* Abigail.) Abigail?

Hale. Excellency, when I first arrived from Beverly, Mr. Parris told me that.

Danforth. Do you deny it, Mr. Parris?

Parris. I do not, sir, but I never saw any of them naked.

Danforth. But she have *danced?*

Parris (*unwillingly*). Aye, sir.

(Danforth, *as though with new eyes, looks at* Abigail.)

Hathorne. Excellency, will you permit me? (*He points at* Mary Warren.)

Danforth (*with great worry*). Pray, proceed.

Hathorne. You say you never saw no spirits, Mary, were never threatened or afflicted by any manifest of the Devil or the Devil's agents.

Mary Warren (*very faintly*). No, sir.

Hathorne (*with a gleam of victory*). And yet, when people accused of witchery confronted you in court, you would faint, saying their spirits came out of their bodies and choked you—

Mary Warren. That were pretense, sir.

Danforth. I cannot hear you.

Mary Warren. Pretense, sir.

Parris. But you did turn cold, did you not? I myself picked you up many times, and your skin were icy. Mr. Danforth, you—

Danforth. I saw that many times.

Proctor. She only pretended to faint, Your Excellency. They're all marvelous pretenders.

Hathorne. Then can she pretend to faint now?

Proctor. Now?

Parris. Why not? Now there are no spirits attacking her, for none in this room is accused of witchcraft. So let her turn herself cold now, let her pretend she is attacked now, let her faint. (*He turns to* Mary Warren.) Faint!

Mary Warren. Faint?

Parris. Aye, faint. Prove to us how you pretended in the court so many times.

Mary Warren (*looking to* Proctor). I—cannot faint now, sir.

Proctor (*alarmed, quietly*). Can you not pretend it?

Mary Warren. I— (*She looks about as though searching for the passion to faint.*) I—have no sense of it now, I—

Danforth. Why? What is lacking now?

Mary Warren. I—cannot tell, sir, I—

Danforth. Might it be that here we have no afflicting spirit loose, but in the court there were some?

Mary Warren. I never saw no spirits.

Parris. Then see no spirits now, and prove to us that you can faint by your own will, as you claim.

Mary Warren (*stares, searching for the emotion of it, and then shakes her head*). I—cannot do it.

Parris. Then you will confess, will you not? It were attacking spirits made you faint!

Mary Warren. No, sir, I—

Parris. Your Excellency, this is a trick to blind the court!

Mary Warren. It's not a trick! (*She stands.*) I—I used to faint because I—I thought I saw spirits.

Danforth. Thought you saw them!

Mary Warren. But I did not, Your Honor.

Hathorne. How could you think you saw them unless you saw them?

Mary Warren. I—I cannot tell how, but I did. I—I heard the other girls screaming, and you, Your Honor, you seemed to believe them, and I—It were only sport in the beginning, sir, but then the whole world cried spirits, spirits, and I—I promise you, Mr. Danforth, I only thought I saw them but I did not.

(Danforth *peers at her.*)

Parris (*smiling, but nervous because* Danforth *seems to be struck by* Mary Warren's *story*). Surely Your Excellency is not taken by this simple lie.

Danforth (*turning worriedly to* Abigail). Abigail. I bid you now search your heart and tell me this—and beware of it, child, to God every soul is precious and His vengeance is terrible on them that take life without cause. Is it possible, child, that the spirits you have seen are illusion only, some deception that may cross your mind when—

Abigail. Why, this—this—is a base question, sir.

Danforth. Child, I would have you consider it—

Abigail. I have been hurt, Mr. Danforth; I have seen my blood runnin' out! I have been near to murdered every day because I done my duty pointing out the Devil's people—and this is my reward? To be mistrusted, denied, questioned like a—

Danforth (*weakening*). Child, I do not mistrust you—

Abigail (*in an open threat*). Let you beware, Mr. Danforth. Think you to be so mighty that the power of Hell may not turn your wits? Beware of it! There is—(*Suddenly, from an accusatory attitude, her face turns, looking into the air above—it is truly frightened.*)

Danforth (*apprehensively*). What is it, child?

Abigail (*looking about in the air, clasping her arms about her as though cold*). I—I know not. A wind, a cold wind, has come. (*Her eyes fall on* Mary Warren.)

Mary Warren (*terrified, pleading*). Abby!

Mercy Lewis (*shivering*). Your Honor, I freeze!

Proctor. They're pretending!

Hathorne (*touching* Abigail's *hand*). She is cold, Your Honor, touch her!

Mercy Lewis (*through chattering teeth*). Mary, do you send this shadow on me?

Mary Warren. Lord, save me!

Susanna Walcott. I freeze, I freeze!

Abigail (*shivering visibly*). It is a wind, a wind!

Mary Warren. Abby, don't do that!

Danforth (*himself engaged and entered by* Abigail). Mary Warren, do you witch her? I say to you, do you send your spirit out?

(*With a hysterical cry* Mary Warren *starts to run.* Proctor *catches her.*)

Mary Warren (*almost collapsing*). Let me go, Mr. Proctor, I cannot, I cannot—

Abigail (*crying to Heaven*). Oh, Heavenly Father, take away this shadow!

(*Without warning or hesitation,* Proctor *leaps at* Abigail *and, grabbing her by the hair, pulls her to her feet. She screams in pain.* Danforth, *astonished, cries, "What are you about?" and* Hathorne *and* Parris *call, "Take your hands off her!" and out of it all comes* Proctor's *roaring voice.*)

Proctor. How do you call Heaven! Whore! Whore!

(Herrick *breaks* Proctor *from her.*)

Herrick. John!

Danforth. Man! Man, what do you—

Proctor (*breathless and in agony*). It is a whore!

Danforth (*dumfounded*). You charge—?

Abigail. Mr. Danforth, he is lying!

Proctor. Mark her! Now she'll suck a scream to stab me with, but—

Danforth. You will prove this! This will not pass!

Proctor (*trembling, his life collapsing about him*). I have known her, sir. I have known her.

Danforth. You—you are a lecher?

Francis (*horrified*). John, you cannot say such a—

Proctor. Oh, Francis, I wish you had some evil in you that you might know me! (*To* Danforth) A man will not cast away his good name. You surely know that.

Danforth (*dumfounded*). In—in what time? In what place?

Proctor (*his voice about to break, and his shame great*). In the proper place—where my beasts are bedded. On the last night of my joy, some eight months past. She used to serve me in my house, sir. (*He has to clamp his jaw to keep from weeping.*) A man may think God sleeps, but God sees everything, I know it now. I beg you, sir, I beg you—see her what she is. My wife, my dear good wife, took this girl soon after, sir, and put her out on the highroad. And being what she is, a lump of vanity, sir—(*He is being overcome.*) Excellency, forgive me, forgive me. (*Angrily against himself, he turns away from the*

Governor *for a moment. Then, as though to cry out is his only means of speech left.*) She thinks to dance with me on my wife's grave! And well she might, for I thought of her softly. God help me, I lusted, and there is a promise in such sweat. But it is a whore's vengeance, and you must see it; I set myself entirely in your hands. I know you must see it now.

Danforth (*blanched, in horror, turning to* Abigail). You deny every scrap and tittle of this?

Abigail. If I must answer that, I will leave and I will not come back again!

(Danforth *seems unsteady.*)

Proctor. I have made a bell of my honor! I have rung the doom of my good name—you will believe me, Mr. Danforth! My wife is innocent, except she knew a whore when she saw one!

Abigail (*stepping up to* Danforth). What look do you give me? (Danforth *cannot speak.*) I'll not have such looks! (*She turns and starts for the door.*)

Danforth. You will remain where you are! (Herrick *steps into her path. She comes up short, fire in her eyes.*) Mr. Parris, go into the court and bring Goodwife Proctor out.

Parris (*objecting*). Your Honor, this is all a—

Danforth (*sharply to* Parris). Bring her out! And tell her not one word of what's been spoken here. And let you knock before you enter. (Parris *goes out.*) Now we shall touch the bottom of this swamp. (*To* Proctor) Your wife, you say, is an honest woman.

Proctor. In her life, sir, she have never lied. There are them that cannot sing, and them that cannot weep — my wife cannot lie. I have paid much to learn it, sir.

Danforth. And when she put this girl out of your house, she put her out for a harlot?

Proctor. Aye, sir.

Danforth. And knew her for a harlot?

Proctor. Aye, sir, she knew her for a harlot.

Danforth. Good then. (*To* Abigail) And if she tell me, child, it were for harlotry, may God spread His mercy on you! (*There is a knock. He calls to the door.*) Hold! (*To* Abigail) Turn your back. Turn your back. (*To* Proctor) Do likewise. (*Both turn their backs—Abigail with indignant slowness.*) Now let neither of you turn to face Goody Proctor. No one in this room is to speak one word, or raise a gesture aye or nay. (*He turns toward the door, calls.*) Enter! (*The door opens. Elizabeth enters with Parris. Parris leaves her. She stands alone, her eyes looking for Proctor.*) Mr. Cheever, report this testimony in all exactness. Are you ready?

Cheever. Ready, sir.

Danforth. Come here, woman. (*Elizabeth comes to him, glancing at Proctor's back.*) Look at me only, not at your husband. In my eyes only.

Elizabeth (*faintly*). Good, sir.

Danforth. We are given to understand that at one time you dismissed your servant, Abigail Williams.

Elizabeth. That is true, sir.

Danforth. For what cause did you dismiss her? (*Slight pause. Then* Elizabeth *tries to glance at* Proctor.) You will look in my eyes only and not at your husband. The answer is in your memory and you need no help to give it to me. Why did you dismiss Abigail Williams?

Elizabeth (*not knowing what to say, sensing a situation, wetting her lips to stall for time*). She—dissatisfied me. (*Pause.*) And my husband.

Danforth. In what way dissatisfied you?

Elizabeth. She were—(*She glances at* Proctor *for a cue.*)

Danforth. Woman, look at me! (Elizabeth *does.*) Were she slovenly? Lazy? What disturbance did she cause?

Elizabeth. Your Honor, I—in that time I were sick. And I—My husband is a good and righteous man. He is never drunk as some are, nor wastin' his time at the shovelboard, but always at his work. But in my sickness—you see, sir, I were a long time sick after my last baby, and I thought I saw my husband somewhat turning from me. And this girl— (*She turns to* Abigail.)

Danforth. Look at me.

Elizabeth. Aye, sir. Abigail Williams—(*She breaks off.*)

Danforth. What of Abigail Williams?

Elizabeth. I came to think he fancied her. And so one night I lost my wits, I think, and put her out on the highroad.

Danforth. Your husband—did he indeed turn from you?

Elizabeth (*in agony*). My husband—is a goodly man, sir.

Danforth. Then he did not turn from you.

Elizabeth (*starting to glance at* Proctor). He—

Danforth (*reaches out and holds her face, then*). Look at me! To your own knowledge, has John Proctor ever committed the crime of lechery? (*In a crisis of indecision she cannot speak.*) Answer my question! Is your husband a lecher!

Elizabeth (*faintly*). No, sir.

Danforth. Remove her, Marshal.

Proctor. Elizabeth, tell the truth!

Danforth. She has spoken. Remove her!

Proctor (*crying out*). Elizabeth, I have confessed it!

Elizabeth. Oh, God! (*The door closes behind her.*)

Proctor. She only thought to save my name!

Hale. Excellency, it is a natural lie to tell; I beg you, stop now before another is condemned! I may shut my conscience to it no more—private vengeance is working through this testimony! From the beginning this man has struck me true. By my oath to Heaven, I believe him now, and I pray you call back his wife before we—

Danforth. She spoke nothing of lechery, and this man has lied!

Hale. I believe him! (*Pointing at* Abigail). This girl has always struck me false! She has—

(Abigail, *with a weird, wild, chilling cry, screams up to the ceiling.*)

Abigail. You will not! Begone! Begone, I say!

Danforth. What is it, child? (*But* Abigail, *pointing with fear, is now raising up her frightened eyes, her awed face, toward the ceiling—the girls are doing the same—and now* Hathorne, Hale, Putnam, Cheever, Herrick, *and* Danforth *do the same.*) What's there? (*He lowers his eyes from the ceiling, and now he is frightened; there is real tension in his voice.*) Child! (*She is transfixed—with all the girls, she is whimpering open-mouthed, agape at the ceiling.*) Girls! Why do you—?

Mercy Lewis (*pointing*). It's on the beam! Behind the rafter!

Danforth (*looking up*). Where!

Abigail. Why—? (*She gulps.*) Why do you come, yellow bird?

Proctor. Where's a bird? I see no bird!

Abigail (*to the ceiling*). My face? My face?

Proctor. Mr. Hale—

Danforth. Be quiet!

Proctor (*to* Hale). Do you see a bird?

Danforth. Be quiet!!

Abigail (*to the ceiling, in a genuine conversation with the "bird," as though trying to talk it out of attacking her*). But God made my face; you cannot want to tear my face. Envy is a deadly sin, Mary.

Mary Warren (*on her feet with a spring, and horrified, pleading*). Abby!

Abigail (*unperturbed, continuing to the "bird"*). Oh, Mary, this is a black art to change your shape. No, I cannot, I cannot stop my mouth; it's God's work I do.

Mary Warren. Abby, I'm here!

Proctor (*frantically*). They're pretending, Mr. Danforth!

Abigail (*now she takes a backward step, as though in fear the bird will swoop down momentarily*). Oh, please, Mary! Don't come down.

Susanna Walcott. Her claws, she's stretching her claws!

Proctor. Lies, lies.

Abigail (*backing further, eyes still fixed above*). Mary, please don't hurt me!

Mary Warren (*to Danforth*). I'm not hurting her!

Danforth (*to Mary Warren*). Why does she see this vision?

Mary Warren. She sees nothin'!

Abigail (*now staring full front as though hypnotized, and mimicking the exact tone of Mary Warren's cry*). She sees nothin'!

Mary Warren (*pleading*). Abby, you mustn't!

Abigail and All the Girls (*all transfixed*). Abby, you mustn't!

Mary Warren (*to all the girls*). I'm here, I'm here!

Girls. I'm here, I'm here!

Danforth (*horrified*). Mary Warren! Draw back your spirit out of them!

Mary Warren. Mr. Danforth!

Girls (*cutting her off*). Mr. Danforth!

Danforth. Have you compacted with the Devil? Have you?

Mary Warren. Never, never!

Girls. Never, never!

Danforth (*growing hysterical*). Why can they only repeat you?

Proctor. Give me a whip—I'll stop it!

Mary Warren. They're sporting. They—!

Girls. They're sporting!

Mary Warren (*turning on them all hysterically and stamping her feet*). Abby, stop it!

Girls (*stamping their feet*). Abby, stop it!

Mary Warren. Stop it!

Girls. Stop it!

Mary Warren (*screaming it out at the top of her lungs, and raising her fists*). Stop it!!

Girls (*raising their fists*). Stop it!!

(Mary Warren, *utterly confounded, and becoming over-whelmed by* Abigail's—*and the girls'—utter conviction, starts to whimper, hands half raised, powerless, and all the girls begin whimpering exactly as she does.*)

Danforth. A little while ago you were afflicted. Now it seems you afflict others; where did you find this power?

Mary Warren (*staring at* Abigail). I—have no power.

Girls. I have no power.

Proctor. They're gulling you, Mister!

Danforth. Why did you turn about this past two weeks? You have seen the Devil, have you not?

Hale (*indicating Abigail and the girls*). You cannot believe them!

Mary Warren. I—

Proctor (*sensing her weakening*). Mary, God damns all liars!

Danforth (*pounding it into her*). You have seen the Devil, you have made compact with Lucifer, have you not?

Proctor. God damns liars, Mary!

(Mary *utters something unintelligible, staring at* Abigail, *who keeps watching the "bird" above.*)

Danforth. I cannot hear you. What do you say? (Mary *utters again unintelligibly.*) You will confess yourself or you will hang! (*He turns her roughly to face him.*) Do you know who I am? I say you will hang if you do not open with me!

Proctor. Mary, remember the angel Raphael—do that which is good and—

Abigail (*pointing upward*). The wings! Her wings are spreading! Mary, please, don't, don't—!

Hale. I see nothing, Your Honor!

Danforth. Do you confess this power! (*He is an inch from her face.*) Speak!

Abigail. She's going to come down! She's walking the beam!

Danforth. Will you speak!

Mary Warren (*staring in horror*). I cannot!

Girls. I cannot!

Parris. Cast the Devil out! Look him in the face! Trample him! We'll save you, Mary, only stand fast against him and—

Abigail (*looking up*). Look out! She's coming down!

(*She and all the girls run to one wall, shielding their eyes. And now, as though cornered, they let out a gigantic scream, and* Mary, *as though infected, opens her mouth and screams with them. Gradually* Abigail *and the girls leave off, until only* Mary *is left there, staring up at the "bird," screaming madly. All watch her, horrified by this evident fit.* Proctor *strides to her.*)

Proctor. Mary, tell the Governor what they— (*He has hardly got a word out, when, seeing him coming for her, she rushes out of his reach, screaming in horror.*)

Mary Warren. Don't touch me—don't touch me! (*At which the girls halt at the door.*)

Proctor (*astonished*). Mary!

Mary Warren (*pointing at* Proctor). You're the Devil's man! (*He is stopped in his tracks.*)

Parris. Praise God!

Girls. Praise God!

Proctor (*numbed*). Mary, how—?

Mary Warren. I'll not hang with you! I love God, I love God.

Danforth (*to* Mary). He bid you do the Devil's work?

Mary Warren (*hysterically, indicating* Proctor). He come at me by night and every day to sign, to sign, to—

Danforth. Sign what?

Parris. The Devil's book? He come with a book?

Mary Warren (*hysterically, pointing at* Proctor, *fearful of him*). My name, he want my name. "I'll murder you," he says, "if my wife hangs! We must go and overthrow the court," he says!

(Danforth's *head jerks toward* Proctor, *shock and horror in his face.*)

Proctor (*turning, appealing to* Hale). Mr. Hale!

Mary Warren (*her sobs beginning*). He wake me every night, his eyes were like coals and his fingers claw my neck, and I sign, I sign . . .

Hale. Excellency, this child's gone wild!

Proctor (*as* Danforth's *wide eyes pour on him*). Mary, Mary!

Mary Warren (*screaming at him*). No, I love God; I go your way no more. I love God, I bless God. (*Sobbing, she rushes to* Abigail.) Abby, Abby, I'll never hurt you more! (*They all watch, as* Abigail, *out of her infinite charity, reaches out and draws the sobbing* Mary *to her, and then looks up to* Danforth.)

Danforth (*to* Proctor). What are you? (Proctor *is beyond speech in his anger.*) You are combined with anti-Christ, are you not? I have seen your power; you will not deny it! What say you, Mister?

Hale. Excellency—

Danforth. I will have nothing from you, Mr. Hale! (*To* Proctor) Will you confess yourself befouled with Hell, or do you keep that black allegiance yet? What say you?

Proctor (*his mind wild, breathless*). I say—I say—God is dead!

Parris. Hear it, hear it!

Proctor (*laughs insanely, then*). A fire, a fire is burning! I hear the boot of Lucifer, I see his filthy face! And it is my face, and yours, Danforth! For them that quail to bring men out of ignorance, as I have quailed, and as you quail now when you know in all your black hearts that this be fraud—God damns our kind especially, and we will burn, we will burn together!

Danforth. Marshal! Take him and Corey with him to the jail!

Hale (*starting across to the door*). I denounce these proceedings!

Proctor. You are pulling Heaven down and raising up a whore!

Hale. I denounce these proceedings, I quit this court! (*He slams the door to the outside behind him.*)

Danforth (*calling to him in a fury*). Mr. Hale! Mr. Hale!

THE CURTAIN FALLS

Act Four

....

(*A cell in Salem jail, that fall.*)

(*At the back is a high barred window; near it, a great, heavy door. Along the walls are two benches.*)

(*The place is in darkness but for the moonlight seeping through the bars. It appears empty. Presently footsteps are heard coming down a corridor beyond the wall, keys rattle, and the door swings open.* Marshal Herrick *enters with a lantern.*)

(*He is nearly drunk, and heavy-footed. He goes to a bench and nudges a bundle of rags lying on it.*)

Herrick. Sarah, wake up! Sarah Good! He then crosses to the other bench.

Sarah Good (*rising in her rags*). Oh, Majesty! Comin', comin'! Tituba, he's here, His Majesty's come!

Herrick. Go to the north cell; this place is wanted now. (*He hangs his lantern on the wall.* Tituba *sits up.*)

Tituba. That don't look to me like His Majesty; look to me like the marshal.

Herrick (*taking out a flask*). Get along with you now, clear this place. (*He drinks, and* Sarah Good *comes and peers up into his face.*)

Sarah Good. Oh, is it you, Marshal! I thought sure you be the devil comin' for us. Could I have a sip of cider for me goin'-away?

Herrick (*handing her the flask*). And where are you off to, Sarah?

Tituba (*as* Sarah *drinks*). We goin' to Barbados, soon the Devil gits here with the feathers and the wings.

Herrick. Oh? A happy voyage to you.

Sarah Good. A pair of bluebirds wingin' southerly, the two of us! Oh, it be a grand transformation, Marshal! (*She raises the flask to drink again.*)

Herrick (*taking the flask from her lips*). You'd best give me that or you'll never rise off the ground. Come along now.

Tituba. I'll speak to him for you, if you desires to come along, Marshal.

Herrick. I'd not refuse it, Tituba; it's the proper morning to fly into Hell.

Tituba. Oh, it be no Hell in Barbados. Devil, him be pleasureman in Barbados, him be singin' and dancin' in Barbados. It's you folks—you riles him up 'round here; it be too cold 'round here for that Old Boy. He freeze his soul in Massachusetts, but in Barbados he just as sweet and—(*A bellowing cow is heard, and* Tituba *leaps up and calls to the window.*) Aye, sir! That's him, Sarah!

Sarah Good. I'm here, Majesty! (*They hurriedly pick up their rags as* Hopkins, *a guard, enters.*)

Hopkins. The Deputy Governor's arrived.

Herrick (*grabbing* Tituba). Come along, come along.

Tituba (*resisting him*). No, he comin' for me. I goin' home!

Herrick (*pulling her to the door*). That's not Satan, just a poor old cow with a hatful of milk. Come along now, out with you!

Tituba (*calling to the window*). Take me home, Devil! Take me home!

Sarah Good (*following the shouting* Tituba *out*). Tell him I'm goin', Tituba! Now you tell him Sarah Good is goin' too!

(*In the corridor outside* Tituba *calls on—"Take me home, Devil; Devil take me home!" and* Hopkins' *voice orders her to move on.* Herrick *returns and begins to push old rags and straw into a corner. Hearing footsteps, he turns, and enter* Danforth *and* Judge Hathorne. *They are in greatcoats and wear hats against the bitter cold. They are followed in by* Cheever, *who carries a dispatch case and a flat wooden box containing his writing materials.*)

Herrick. Good morning, Excellency.

Danforth. Where is Mr. Parris?

Herrick. I'll fetch him. (*He starts for the door.*)

Danforth. Marshal. (Herrick *stops.*) When did Reverend Hale arrive?

Herrick. It were toward midnight, I think.

Danforth (*suspiciously*). What is he about here?

Herrick. He goes among them that will hang, sir. And he prays with them. He sits with Goody Nurse now. And Mr. Parris with him.

Danforth. Indeed. That man have no authority to enter here, Marshal. Why have you let him in?

Herrick. Why, Mr. Parris command me, sir. I cannot deny him.

Danforth. Are you drunk, Marshal?

Herrick. No, sir; it is a bitter night, and I have no fire here.

Danforth (*containing his anger*). Fetch Mr. Parris.

Herrick. Aye, sir.

Danforth. There is a prodigious stench in this place.

Herrick. I have only now cleared the people out for you.

Danforth. Beware hard drink, Marshal.

Herrick. Aye, sir. (*He waits an instant for further orders. But* Danforth, *in dissatisfaction, turns his back on him, and* Herrick *goes out. There is a pause.* Danforth *stands in thought.*)

Hathorne. Let you question Hale, Excellency; I should not be surprised he have been preaching in Andover lately.

Danforth. We'll come to that; speak nothing of Andover. Parris prays with him. That's strange. (*He blows on his hands, moves toward the window, and looks out.*)

Hathorne. Excellency, I wonder if it be wise to let Mr. Parris so continuously with the prisoners. (Danforth *turns to him, interested.*) I think, sometimes, the man has a mad look these days.

Danforth. Mad?

Hathorne. I met him yesterday coming out of his house, and I bid him good morning—and he wept and went his way. I think it is not well the village sees him so unsteady.

Danforth. Perhaps he have some sorrow.

Cheever (*stamping his feet against the cold*). I think it be the cows, sir.

Danforth. Cows?

Cheever. There be so many cows wanderin' the high-roads, now their masters are in the jails, and much disagreement who they will belong to now. I know Mr. Parris be arguin' with farmers all yesterday—there is great contention, sir, about the cows. Contention make him weep, sir; it were always a man that weep for contention. (*He turns, as do* Hathorne *and* Danforth, *hearing someone coming up the corridor.* Danforth *raises his head as* Parris *enters. He is gaunt, frightened, and sweating in his greatcoat.*)

Parris (*to* Danforth, *instantly*). Oh, good morning, sir, thank you for coming, I beg your pardon wakin' you so early. Good morning, Judge Hathorne.

Danforth. Reverend Hale have no right to enter this—

Parris. Excellency, a moment. (*He hurries back and shuts the door.*)

Hathorne. Do you leave him alone with the prisoners?

Danforth. What's his business here?

Parris (*prayerfully holding up his hands*). Excellency, hear me. It is a providence. Reverend Hale has returned to bring Rebecca Nurse to God.

Danforth (*surprised*). He bids her confess?

Parris (*sitting*). Hear me. Rebecca have not given me a word this three month since she came. Now she sits with him, and her sister and Martha Corey and two or three others, and he pleads with them, confess their crimes and save their lives.

Danforth. Why—this is indeed a providence. And they soften, they soften?

Parris. Not yet, not yet. But I thought to summon you, sir, that we might think on whether it be not wise, to—(*He dares not say it.*) I had thought to put a question, sir, and I hope you will not—

Danforth. Mr. Parris, be plain, what troubles you?

Parris. There is news, sir, that the court—the court must reckon with. My niece, sir, my niece—I believe she has vanished.

Danforth. Vanished!

Parris. I had thought to advise you of it earlier in the week, but—

Danforth. Why? How long is she gone?

Parris. This be the third night. You see, sir, she told me she would stay a night with Mercy Lewis. And next day, when she does not return, I send to Mr. Lewis to inquire. Mercy told him she would sleep in *my* house for a night.

Danforth. They are both gone?!

Parris (*in fear of him*). They are, sir.

Danforth (*alarmed*). I will send a party for them. Where may they be?

Parris. Excellency, I think they be aboard a ship. (Danforth *stands agape.*) My daughter tells me how she heard them speaking of ships last week, and tonight I discover my—my strongbox is broke into. (*He presses his fingers against his eyes to keep back tears.*)

Hathorne (*astonished*). She have robbed you?

Parris. Thirty-one pound is gone. I am penniless. (*He covers his face and sobs.*)

Danforth. Mr. Parris, you are a brainless man! (*He walks in thought, deeply worried.*)

Parris. Excellency, it profit nothing you should blame me. I cannot think they would run off except they fear to keep in Salem any more. (*He is pleading.*) Mark it, sir, Abigail had close knowledge of the town, and since the news of Andover has broken here—

Danforth. Andover is remedied. The court returns there on Friday, and will resume examinations.

Parris. I am sure of it, sir. But the rumor here speaks rebellion in Andover, and it—

Danforth. There is no rebellion in Andover!

Parris. I tell you what is said here, sir. Andover have thrown out the court, they say, and will have no part of witchcraft. There be a faction here, feeding on that news, and I tell you true, sir, I fear there will be riot here.

Hathorne. Riot! Why at every execution I have seen naught but high satisfaction in the town.

Parris. Judge Hathorne—it were another sort that hanged till now. Rebecca Nurse is no Bridget that lived three year with Bishop before she married him. John Proctor is not Isaac Ward that drank his family to ruin. (*To* Danforth) I would to God it were not so, Excellency, but these people have great weight yet in the town. Let Rebecca stand upon the gibbet and send up some righteous prayer, and I fear she'll wake a vengeance on you.

Hathorne. Excellency, she is condemned a witch. The court have—

Danforth (*in deep concern, raising a hand to* Hathorne). Pray you. (*To* Parris.) How do you propose, then?

Parris. Excellency, I would postpone these hangin's for a time.

Danforth. There will be no postponement.

Parris. Now Mr. Hale's returned, there is hope, I think —for if he bring even one of these to God, that confession surely damns the others in the public eye, and none may doubt more that they are all linked to Hell. This way, unconfessed and claiming innocence, doubts are multiplied, many honest people will weep for them, and our good purpose is lost in their tears.

Danforth (*after thinking a moment, then going to* Cheever). Give me the list.

(Cheever *opens the dispatch case, searches.*)

Parris. It cannot be forgot, sir, that when I summoned the congregation for John Proctor's excommunication there were hardly thirty people come to hear it. That speak a discontent, I think, and—

Danforth (*studying the list*). There will be no postponement.

Parris. Excellency—

Danforth. Now, sir—which of these in your opinion may be brought to God? I will myself strive with him till dawn. (*He hands the list to* Parris, *who merely glances at it.*)

Parris. There is not sufficient time till dawn.

Danforth. I shall do my utmost. Which of them do you have hope for?

Parris (*not even glancing at the list now, and in a quavering voice, quietly*). Excellency—a dagger—(*He chokes up.*)

Danforth. What do you say?

Parris. Tonight, when I open my door to leave my house—a dagger clattered to the ground. (*Silence. Danforth absorbs this. Now Parris cries out.*) You cannot hang this sort. There is danger for me. I dare not step outside at night!

(*Reverend Hale enters. They look at him for an instant in silence. He is steeped in sorrow, exhausted, and more direct than he ever was.*)

Danforth. Accept my congratulations, Reverend Hale; we are gladdened to see you returned to your good work.

Hale (*coming to Danforth now*). You must pardon them. They will not budge.

(*Herrick enters, waits.*)

Danforth (*conciliatory*). You misunderstand, sir; I cannot pardon these when twelve are already hanged for the same crime. It is not just.

Parris (*with failing heart*). Rebecca will not confess?

Hale. The sun will rise in a few minutes. Excellency, I must have more time.

Danforth. Now hear me, and beguile yourselves no more. I will not receive a single plea for pardon or postponement. Them that will not confess will hang. Twelve are already executed; the names of these seven are given out, and the village expects to see them die this morning. Postponement now speaks a floundering on my part; reprieve or pardon must cast doubt upon the guilt of them that died till now. While I speak God's law, I will not crack its voice with whimpering. If retaliation is your fear, know this—I should hang ten thousand that dared to rise against the law, and an ocean of salt tears could not melt the resolution of the statutes. Now draw yourselves up like men and help me, as you are bound by Heaven to do. Have you spoken with them all, Mr. Hale?

Hale. All but Proctor. He is in the dungeon.

Danforth (*to* Herrick). What's Proctor's way now?

Herrick. He sits like some great bird; you'd not know he lived except he will take food from time to time.

Danforth (*after thinking a moment*). His wife—his wife must be well on with child now.

Herrick. She is, sir.

Danforth. What think you, Mr. Parris? You have closer knowledge of this man; might her presence soften him?

Parris. It is possible, sir. He have not laid eyes on her these three months. I should summon her.

Danforth (*to Herrick*). Is he yet adamant? Has he struck at you again?

Herrick. He cannot, sir, he is chained to the wall now.

Danforth (*after thinking on it*). Fetch Goody Proctor to me. Then let you bring him up.

Herrick. Aye, sir. (Herrick *goes. There is silence.*)

Hale. Excellency, if you postpone a week and publish to the town that you are striving for their confessions, that speak mercy on your part, not faltering.

Danforth. Mr. Hale, as God have not empowered me like Joshua to stop this sun from rising, so I cannot withhold from them the perfection of their punishment.

Hale (*harder now*). If you think God wills you to raise rebellion, Mr. Danforth, you are mistaken!

Danforth (*instantly*). You have heard rebellion spoken in the town?

Hale. Excellency, there are orphans wandering from house to house; abandoned cattle bellow on the highroads, the stink of rotting crops hangs everywhere, and no man knows when the harlots' cry will end his life—and you wonder yet if rebellion's spoke? Better you should marvel how they do not burn your province!

Danforth. Mr. Hale, have you preached in Andover this month?

Hale. Thank God they have no need of me in Andover.

Danforth. You baffle me, sir. Why have you returned here?

Hale. Why, it is all simple. I come to do the Devil's work. I come to counsel Christians they should belie themselves. (*His sarcasm collapses.*) There is blood on my head! Can you not see the blood on my head!!

Parris. Hush! (*For he has heard footsteps. They all face the door.* Herrick *enters with* Elizabeth. *Her wrists are linked by heavy chain, which* Herrick *now removes. Her clothes are dirty; her face is pale and gaunt.* Herrick *goes out.*)

Danforth (*very politely*). Goody Proctor. (*She is silent.*) I hope you are hearty?

Elizabeth (*as a warning reminder*). I am yet six month before my time.

Danforth. Pray be at your ease, we come not for your life. We—(*uncertain how to plead, for he is not accustomed to it.*) Mr. Hale, will you speak with the woman?

Hale. Goody Proctor, your husband is marked to hang this morning.

(*Pause.*)

Elizabeth (*quietly*). I have heard it.

Hale. You know, do you not, that I have no connection with the court? (*She seems to doubt it.*) I come of my own, Goody Proctor. I would save your husband's life, for if he is taken I count myself his murderer. Do you understand me?

Elizabeth. What do you want of me?

Hale. Goody Proctor, I have gone this three month like our Lord into the wilderness. I have sought a Christian way, for damnation's doubled on a minister who counsels men to lie.

Hathorne. It is no lie, you cannot speak of lies.

Hale. It is a lie! They are innocent!

Danforth. I'll hear no more of that!

Hale (*continuing to* Elizabeth). Let you not mistake your duty as I mistook my own. I came into this village like a bridegroom to his beloved, bearing gifts of high religion; the very crowns of holy law I brought, and what I touched with my bright confidence, it died; and where I turned the eye of my great faith, blood flowed up. Beware, Goody Proctor—cleave to no faith when faith brings blood. It is mistaken law that leads you to sacrifice. Life, woman, life is God's most precious gift; no principle, however glorious, may justify the taking of it. I beg you, woman, prevail upon your husband to confess. Let him give his lie. Quail not before God's judgment in this, for it may well be God damns a liar less than he that throws his life away for pride. Will you plead with him? I cannot think he will listen to another.

Elizabeth (*quietly*). I think that be the Devil's argument.

Hale (*with a climactic desperation*). Woman, before the laws of God we are as swine! We cannot read His will!

Elizabeth. I cannot dispute with you, sir; I lack learning for it.

Danforth (*going to her*). Goody Proctor, you are not summoned here for disputation. Be there no wifely tenderness within you? He will die with the sunrise. Your husband. Do you understand it? (*She only looks at him.*) What say you? Will you contend with him? (*She is silent.*) Are you stone? I tell you true, woman, had I no other proof of your unnatural life, your dry eyes now would be sufficient evidence that you delivered up your soul to Hell! A very ape would weep at such calamity! Have the devil dried up any tear of pity in you? (*She is silent.*) Take her out. It profit nothing she should speak to him!

Elizabeth (*quietly*). Let me speak with him, Excellency.

Parris (*with hope*). You'll strive with him? (*She hesitates.*)

Danforth. Will you plead for his confession or will you not?

Elizabeth. I promise nothing. Let me speak with him.

(*A sound—the sibilance of dragging feet on stone. They turn. A pause.* Herrick *enters with* John Proctor. *His wrists are chained. He is another man, bearded, filthy, his eyes misty as though webs had overgrown them. He halts inside the doorway, his eye caught by the sight of* Elizabeth. *The emotion flowing between them prevents anyone from speaking for an instant. Now* Hale, *visibly affected, goes to* Danforth *and speaks quietly.*)

Hale. Pray, leave them, Excellency.

Danforth (*pressing* Hale *impatiently aside*). Mr. Proctor, you have been notified, have you not? (Proctor *is silent, staring at* Elizabeth.) I see light in the sky, Mister; let you counsel with your wife, and may God help you turn your back on Hell. (Proctor *is silent, staring at* Elizabeth.)

Hale (*quietly*). Excellency, let—

(Danforth *brushes past* Hale *and walks out.* Hale *follows.* Cheever *stands and follows,* Hathorne *behind.* Herrick *goes.* Parris, *from a safe distance, offers*)

Parris. If you desire a cup of cider, Mr. Proctor, I am sure I—(Proctor *turns an icy stare at him, and he breaks off.* Parris *raises his palms toward* Proctor.) God lead you now. (Parris *goes out.*)

(*Alone.* Proctor *walks to her, halts. It is as though they stood in a spinning world. It is beyond sorrow, above it. He reaches out his hand as though toward an embodiment not quite real, and as he touches her, a strange soft sound, half laughter, half amazement, comes from his throat. He pats her hand. She covers his hand with hers. And then, weak, he sits. Then she sits, facing him.*)

Proctor. The child?

Elizabeth. It grows.

Proctor. There is no word of the boys?

Elizabeth. They're well. Rebecca's Samuel keeps them.

Proctor. You have not seen them?

Elizabeth. I have not. (*She catches a weakening in herself and downs it.*)

Proctor. You are a—marvel, Elizabeth.

Elizabeth. You—have been tortured?

Proctor. Aye. (*Pause. She will not let herself be drowned in the sea that threatens her.*) They come for my life now.

Elizabeth. I know it.

(*Pause.*)

Proctor. None—have yet confessed?

Elizabeth. There be many confessed.

Proctor. Who are they?

Elizabeth. There be a hundred or more, they say. Goody Ballard is one; Isaiah Goodkind is one. There be many.

Proctor. Rebecca?

Elizabeth. Not Rebecca. She is one foot in Heaven now; naught may hurt her more.

Proctor. And Giles?

Elizabeth. You have not heard of it?

Proctor. I hear nothin', where I am kept.

Elizabeth. Giles is dead.

(*He looks at her incredulously.*)

Proctor. When were he hanged?

Elizabeth (*quietly, factually*). He were not hanged. He would not answer aye or nay to his indictment; for if he denied the charge they'd hang him surely, and auction out his property. So he stand mute, and died Christian under the law. And so his sons will have his farm. It is the law, for he could not be condemned a wizard without he answer the indictment, aye or nay.

Proctor. Then how does he die?

Elizabeth (*gently*). They press him, John.

Proctor. Press?

Elizabeth. Great stones they lay upon his chest until he plead aye or nay. (*With a tender smile for the old man.*) They say he give them but two words. "More weight," he says. And died.

Proctor (*numbed—a thread to weave into his agony*). "More weight."

Elizabeth. Aye. It were a fearsome man, Giles Corey.

(*Pause.*)

Proctor (*with great force of will, but not quite looking at her*). I have been thinking I would confess to them, Elizabeth. (*She shows nothing.*) What say you? If I give them that?

Elizabeth. I cannot judge you, John.

(*Pause.*)

Proctor (*simply—a pure question*). What would you have me do?

Elizabeth. As you will, I would have it. (*Slight pause.*) I want you living, John. That's sure.

Proctor (*pauses, then with a flailing of hope*). Giles' wife? Have she confessed?

Elizabeth. She will not.

(*Pause.*)

Proctor. It is a pretense, Elizabeth.

Elizabeth. What is?

Proctor. I cannot mount the gibbet like a saint. It is a fraud. I am not that man. (*She is silent.*) My honesty is broke, Elizabeth; I am no good man. Nothing's spoiled by giving them this lie that were not rotten long before.

Elizabeth. And yet you've not confessed till now. That speak goodness in you.

Proctor. Spite only keeps me silent. It is hard to give a lie to dogs. (*Pause, for the first time he turns directly to her.*) I would have your forgiveness, Elizabeth.

Elizabeth. It is not for me to give, John, I am—

Proctor. I'd have you see some honesty in it. Let them that never lied die now to keep their souls. It is pretense for me, a vanity that will not blind God nor keep my children out of the wind. (*Pause.*) What say you?

Elizabeth (*upon a heaving sob that always threatens*). John, it come to naught that I should forgive you, if you'll not forgive yourself. (*Now he turns away a little, in great agony.*) It is not my soul, John, it is yours. (*He stands, as though in physical pain, slowly rising to his feet with a great immortal longing to find his answer. It is difficult to say, and she is on the verge of tears.*) Only be sure of this, for I know it now: Whatever you will do, it is a good man does it. (*He turns his doubting, searching gaze upon her.*) I have read my heart this three month, John. (*Pause.*) I have sins of my own to count. It needs a cold wife to prompt lechery.

Proctor (*in great pain*). Enough, enough—

Elizabeth (*now pouring out her heart*). Better you should know me!

Proctor. I will not hear it! I know you!

Elizabeth. You take my sins upon you, John—

Proctor (*in agony*). No, I take my own, my own!

Elizabeth. John, I counted myself so plain, so poorly made, no honest love could come to me! Suspicion kissed you when I did; I never knew how I should say my love. It were a cold house I kept! (*In fright, she swerves, as* Hathorne *enters.*)

Hathorne. What say you, Proctor? The sun is soon up.

(Proctor, *his chest heaving, stares, turns to* Elizabeth. *She comes to him as though to plead, her voice quaking.*)

Elizabeth. Do what you will. But let none be your judge. There be no higher judge under Heaven than Proctor is! Forgive me, forgive me, John—I never knew such goodness in the world! (*She covers her face, weeping.*)

(Proctor *turns from her to* Hathorne; *he is off the earth, his voice hollow.*)

Proctor. I want my life.

Hathorne (*electrified, surprised*). You'll confess yourself?

Proctor. I will have my life.

Hathorne (*with a mystical tone*). God be praised! It is a providence! (*He rushes out the door, and his voice is heard calling down the corridor.*) He will confess! Proctor will confess!

Proctor (*with a cry, as he strides to the door*). Why do you cry it? (*In great pain he turns back to her.*) It is evil, is it not? It is evil.

Elizabeth (*in terror, weeping*). I cannot judge you, John, I cannot!

Proctor. Then who will judge me? (*Suddenly clasping his hands.*) God in Heaven, what is John Proctor, what is John Proctor? (*He moves as an animal, and a fury is riding in him, a tantalized search.*) I think it is honest, I think so; I am no saint. (*As though she had denied this he calls angrily at her.*) Let Rebecca go like a saint; for me it is fraud!

(*Voices are heard in the hall, speaking together in suppressed excitement.*)

Elizabeth. I am not your judge, I cannot be. (*As though giving him release.*) Do as you will, do as you will!

Proctor. Would you give them such a lie? Say it. Would you ever give them this? (*She cannot answer.*) You would not; if tongs of fire were singeing you you would not! It is evil. Good, then—it is evil, and I do it!

(Hathorne *enters with* Danforth, *and, with them,* Cheever, Parris, *and* Hale. *It is a businesslike, rapid entrance, as though the ice had been broken.*)

Danforth (*with great relief and gratitude*). Praise to God, man, praise to God; you shall be blessed in Heaven for this. (Cheever *has hurried to the bench with pen, ink, and paper.* Proctor *watches him.*) Now then, let us have it. Are you ready, Mr. Cheever?

Proctor (*with a cold, cold horror at their efficiency*). Why must it be written?

Danforth. Why, for the good instruction of the village, Mister; this we shall post upon the church door! (*To* Parris, *urgently.*) Where is the marshal?

Parris (*runs to the door and calls down the corridor*). Marshal! Hurry!

Danforth. Now, then, Mister, will you speak slowly, and directly to the point, for Mr. Cheever's sake. (*He is on record now, and is really dictating to* Cheever, *who writes.*) Mr. Proctor, have you seen the Devil in your life? (Proctor's *jaws lock.*) Come, man, there is light in the sky; the town waits at the scaffold; I would give out this news. Did you see the Devil?

Proctor. I did.

Parris. Praise God!

Danforth. And when he come to you, what were his demand? (Proctor *is silent.* Danforth *helps.*) Did he bid you to do his work upon the earth?

Proctor. He did.

Danforth. And you bound yourself to his service? (Danforth *turns, as* Rebecca Nurse *enters, with* Herrick *helping to support her. She is barely able to walk.*) Come in, come in, woman!

Rebecca (*brightening as she sees* Proctor). Ah, John! You are well, then, eh?

(Proctor *turns his face to the wall.*)

Danforth. Courage, man, courage—let her witness your good example that she may come to God herself. Now hear it, Goody Nurse! Say on, Mr. Proctor. Did you bind yourself to the Devil's service?

Rebecca (*astonished*). Why, John!

Proctor (*through his teeth, his face turned from* Rebecca). I did.

Danforth. Now, woman, you surely see it profit nothin' to keep this conspiracy any further. Will you confess yourself with him?

Rebecca. Oh, John—God send his mercy on you!

Danforth. I say, will you confess yourself, Goody Nurse?

Rebecca. Why, it is a lie, it is a lie; how may I damn myself? I cannot, I cannot.

Danforth. Mr. Proctor. When the Devil came to you did you see Rebecca Nurse in his company? (Proctor *is silent.*) Come, man, take courage—did you ever see her with the Devil?

Proctor (*almost inaudibly*). No.

(Danforth, *now sensing trouble, glances at* John *and goes to the table, and picks up a sheet—the list of condemned.*)

Danforth. Did you ever see her sister, Mary Easty, with the Devil?

Proctor. No, I did not.

Danforth (*his eyes narrow on* Proctor). Did you ever see Martha Corey with the Devil?

Proctor. I did not.

Danforth (*realizing, slowly putting the sheet down*). Did you ever see anyone with the Devil?

Proctor. I did not.

Danforth. Proctor, you mistake me. I am not empowered to trade your life for a lie. You have most certainly seen some person with the Devil. (Proctor *is silent.*) Mr. Proctor, a score of people have already testified they saw this woman with the Devil.

Proctor. Then it is proved. Why must I say it?

Danforth. Why "must" you say it! Why, you should rejoice to say it if your soul is truly purged of any love for Hell!

Proctor. They think to go like saints. I like not to spoil their names.

Danforth (*inquiring, incredulous*). Mr. Proctor, do you think they go like saints?

Proctor (*evading*). This woman never thought she done the Devil's work.

Danforth. Look you, sir. I think you mistake your duty here. It matters nothing what she thought—she is convicted of the unnatural murder of children, and you for sending your spirit out upon Mary Warren. Your soul alone is the issue here, Mister, and you will prove its whiteness or you cannot live in a Christian country. Will you tell me now what persons conspired with you in the Devil's company? (*Proctor is silent.*) To your knowledge was Rebecca Nurse ever—

Proctor. I speak my own sins; I cannot judge another. (*Crying out, with hatred*) I have no tongue for it.

Hale (*quickly to* Danforth). Excellency, it is enough he confess himself. Let him sign it, let him sign it.

Parris (*feverishly*). It is a great service, sir. It is a weighty name; it will strike the village that Proctor confess. I beg you, let him sign it. The sun is up, Excellency!

Danforth (*considers; then with dissatisfaction*). Come, then, sign your testimony. (*To* Cheever) Give it to him. (*Cheever goes to* Proctor, *the confession and a pen in hand.* Proctor *does not look at it.*) Come, man, sign it.

Proctor (*after glancing at the confession*). You have all witnessed it—it is enough.

Danforth. You will not sign it?

Proctor. You have all witnessed it; what more is needed?

Danforth. Do you sport with me? You will sign your name or it is no confession, Mister! (*His breast heaving with agonized breathing,* Proctor *now lays the paper down and signs his name.*)

Parris. Praise be to the Lord!

(Proctor *has just finished signing when* Danforth *reaches for the paper. But* Proctor *snatches it up, and now a wild terror is rising in him, and a boundless anger.*)

Danforth (*perplexed, but politely extending his hand*). If you please, sir.

Proctor. No.

Danforth (*as though* Proctor *did not understand*). Mr. Proctor, I must have—

Proctor. No, no. I have signed it. You have seen me. It is done! You have no need for this.

Parris. Proctor, the village must have proof that—

Proctor. Damn the village! I confess to God, and God has seen my name on this! It is enough!

Danforth. No, sir, it is—

Proctor. You came to save my soul, did you not? Here! I have confessed myself; it is enough!

Danforth. You have not con—

Proctor. I have confessed myself! Is there no good penitence but it be public? God does not need my name nailed upon the church! God sees my name; God knows how black my sins are! It is enough!

Danforth. Mr. Proctor—

Proctor. You will not use me! I am no Sarah Good or Tituba, I am John Proctor! You will not use me! It is no part of salvation that you should use me!

Danforth. I do not wish to—

Proctor. I have three children—how may I teach them to walk like men in the world, and I sold my friends?

Danforth. You have not sold your friends—

Proctor. Beguile me not! I blacken all of them when this is nailed to the church the very day they hang for silence!

Danforth. Mr. Proctor, I must have good and legal proof that you—

Proctor. You are the high court, your word is good enough! Tell them I confessed myself; say Proctor broke his knees and wept like a woman; say what you will, but my name cannot—

Danforth (*with suspicion*). It is the same, is it not? If I report it or you sign to it?

Proctor (*he knows it is insane*). No, it is not the same! What others say and what I sign to is not the same!

Danforth. Why? Do you mean to deny this confession when you are free?

Proctor. I mean to deny nothing!

Danforth. Then explain to me, Mr. Proctor, why you will not let—

Proctor (*with a cry of his whole soul*). Because it is my name! Because I cannot have another in my life! Because I lie and sign myself to lies! Because I am not worth the dust on the feet of them that hang! How may I live without my name? I have given you my soul; leave me my name!

Danforth (*pointing at the confession in* Proctor's *hand*). Is that document a lie? If it is a lie I will not accept it! What say you? I will not deal in lies, Mister! (Proctor *is motionless.*) You will give me your honest confession in my hand, or I cannot keep you from the rope. (Proctor *does not reply.*) Which way do you go, Mister?

(*His breast heaving, his eyes staring,* Proctor *tears the paper and crumples it, and he is weeping in fury, but erect.*)

Danforth. Marshal!

Parris (*hysterically, as though the tearing paper were his life*). Proctor, Proctor!

Hale. Man, you will hang! You cannot!

Proctor (*his eyes full of tears*). I can. And there's your first marvel, that I can. You have made your magic now, for now I do think I see some shred of goodness in John Proctor. Not enough to weave a banner with, but white enough to keep it from such dogs. (Elizabeth, *in a burst of terror, rushes to him and weeps against his hand.*) Give them no tear! Tears pleasure them! Show honor now, show a stony heart and sink them with it! (*He has lifted her, and kisses her now with great passion.*)

Rebecca. Let you fear nothing! Another judgment waits us all!

Danforth. Hang them high over the town! Who weeps for these, weeps for corruption! (*He sweeps out past them.* Herrick *starts to lead* Rebecca, *who almost collapses, but* Proctor *catches her, and she glances up at him apologetically.*)

Rebecca. I've had no breakfast.

Herrick. Come, man.

(Herrick *escorts them out,* Hathorne *and* Cheever *behind them.* Elizabeth *stands staring at the empty doorway.*)

Parris (*in deadly fear, to* Elizabeth). Go to him, Goody Proctor! There is yet time!

(*From outside a drumroll strikes the air.* Parris *is startled.* Elizabeth *jerks about toward the window.*)

Parris. Go to him! (*He rushes out the door, as though to hold back his fate.*) Proctor! Proctor!

(*Again, a short burst of drums.*)

Hale. Woman, plead with him! (*He starts to rush out the door, and then goes back to her.*) Woman! It is pride, it is vanity. (*She avoids his eyes, and moves to the window. He drops to his knees.*) Be his helper!—What profit him to bleed? Shall the dust praise him? Shall the worms declare his truth? Go to him, take his shame away!

Elizabeth (*supporting herself against collapse, grips the bars of the window, and with a cry*). He have his goodness now. God forbid I take it from him!

(*The final drumroll crashes, then heightens violently.* Hale *weeps in frantic prayer, and the new sun is pouring in upon her face, and the drums rattle like bones in the morning air.*)

THE CURTAIN FALLS

ECHOES DOWN THE CORRIDOR

Not long after the fever died, Parris was voted from office, walked out on the highroad, and was never heard of again.

The legend has it that Abigail turned up later as a prostitute in Boston.

Twenty years after the last execution, the government awarded compensation to the victims still living, and to the families of the dead. However, it is evident that some people still were unwilling to admit their total guilt, and also that the factionalism was still alive, for some beneficiaries were actually not victims at all, but informers.

Elizabeth Proctor married again, four years after Proctor's death.

In solemn meeting, the congregation rescinded the excommunications—this in March 1712. But they did so upon orders of the government. The jury, however, wrote a statement praying forgiveness of all who had suffered.

Certain farms which had belonged to the victims were left to ruin, and for more than a century no one would buy them or live on them.

To all intents and purposes, the power of theocracy in Massachusetts was broken.

APPENDIX

Act Two, Scene 2

(*A wood. Night.*)

(Proctor *enters with lantern, glowing behind him, then halts, holding lantern raised.* Abigail *appears with a wrap over her nightgown, her hair down. A moment of questioning silence.*)

Proctor (*searching*). I must speak with you, Abigail. (*She does not move, staring at him.*) Will you sit?

Abigail. How do you come?

Proctor. Friendly.

Abigail (*glancing about*). I don't like the woods at night. Pray you, stand closer. (*He comes closer to her.*) I knew it must be you. When I heard the pebbles on the window, before I opened up my eyes I knew. (*Sits on log.*) I thought you would come a good time sooner.

Proctor. I had thought to come many times.

Abigail. Why didn't you? I am so alone in the world now.

Proctor (*as a fact, not bitterly*). Are you! I've heard that people ride a hundred mile to see your face these days.

Abigail. Aye, my face. Can you see my face?

Proctor (*holds lantern to her face*). Then you're troubled?

Abigail. Have you come to mock me?

Proctor (*sets lantern on ground. Sits next to her*). No, no, but I hear only that you go to the tavern every night, and play shovelboard with the Deputy Governor, and they give you cider.

Abigail. I have once or twice played the shovelboard. But I have no joy in it.

Proctor. This is a surprise, Abby. I'd thought to find you gayer than this. I'm told a troop of boys go step for step with you wherever you walk these days.

Abigail. Aye, they do. But I have only lewd looks from the boys.

Proctor. And you like that not?

Abigail. I cannot bear lewd looks no more, John. My spirit's changed entirely. I ought be given Godly looks when I suffer for them as I do.

Proctor. Oh? How do you suffer, Abby?

Abigail (*pulls up dress*). Why, look at my leg. I'm holes all over from their damned needles and pins. (*Touching her stomach*). The jab your wife gave me's not healed yet, y'know.

Proctor (*seeing her madness now*). Oh, it isn't.

Abigail. I think sometimes she pricks it open again while I sleep.

Proctor. Ah?

Abigail. And George Jacobs—(*sliding up her sleeve*)—he comes again and again and raps me with his stick —the same spot every night all this week. Look at the lump I have.

Proctor. Abby—George Jacobs is in the jail all this month.

Abigail. Thank God he is, and bless the day he hangs and lets me sleep in peace again! Oh, John, the world's so full of hypocrites! (*Astonished, outraged.*) They pray in jail! I'm told they all pray in jail!

Proctor. They may not pray?

Abigail. And torture me in my bed while sacred words are comin' from their mouths? Oh, it will need God Himself to cleanse this town properly!

Proctor. Abby—you mean to cry out still others?

Abigail. If I live, if I am not murdered, I surely will, until the last hypocrite is dead.

Proctor. Then there is no good?

Abigail. Aye, there is one. You are good.

Proctor. Am I! How am I good?

Abigail. Why, you taught me goodness, therefore you are good. It were a fire you walked me through, and all my ignorance was burned away. It were a fire, John, we lay in fire. And from that night no woman dare call me wicked any more but I knew my answer. I used to weep for my sins when the wind lifted up my skirts; and blushed for shame because some old Rebecca called me loose. And then you burned my ignorance away. As bare as some December tree I saw them all—walking like saints to church, running to feed the sick, and hypocrites in their hearts! And God gave me strength to call them liars, and God made men to listen to me, and by God I will scrub the world clean for the love of Him! Oh, John, I will make you such a wife when the world is white again! (*She kisses his hand.*) You will be amazed to see me every day, a light of heaven in your house, a—(*He rises, backs away amazed.*) Why are you cold?

Proctor. My wife goes to trial in the morning, Abigail.

Abigail (*distantly*). Your wife?

Proctor. Surely you knew of it?

Abigail. I do remember it now. How—how—Is she well?

Proctor. As well as she may be, thirty-six days in that place.

Abigail. You said you came friendly.

Proctor. She will not be condemned, Abby.

Abigail. You brought me from my bed to speak of her?

Proctor. I come to tell you, Abby, what I will do tomorrow in the court. I would not take you by surprise, but give you all good time to think on what to do to save yourself.

Abigail. Save myself!

Proctor. If you do not free my wife tomorrow, I am set and bound to ruin you, Abby.

Abigail (*her voice small—astonished*). How—ruin me?

Proctor. I have rocky proof in documents that you knew that poppet were none of my wife's; and that you yourself bade Mary Warren stab that needle into it.

Abigail (*a wildness stirs in her, a child is standing here who is unutterably frustrated, denied her wish, but she is still grasping for her wits*). I bade Mary Warren—?

Proctor. You know what you do, you are not so mad!

Abigail. Oh, hypocrites! Have you won him, too? John, why do you let them send you?

Proctor. I warn you, Abby!

Abigail. They send you! They steal your honesty and—

Proctor. I have found my honesty!

Abigail. No, this is your wife pleading, your sniveling, envious wife! This is Rebecca's voice, Martha Corey's voice. You were no hypocrite!

Proctor. I will prove you for the fraud you are!

Abigail. And if they ask you why Abigail would ever do so murderous a deed, what will you tell them?

Proctor. I will tell them why.

Abigail. What will you tell? You will confess to fornication? In the court?

Proctor. If you will have it so, so I will tell it! (*She utters a disbelieving laugh.*) I say I will! (*She laughs louder, now with more assurance he will never do it. He shakes her roughly.*) If you can still hear, hear this! Can you hear! (*She is trembling, staring up at him as though he were out of his mind.*) You will tell the court you are blind to spirits; you cannot see them any more, and you will never cry witchery again, or I will make you famous for the whore you are!

Abigail (*grabs him*). Never in this world! I know you, John—you are this moment singing secret hallelujahs that your wife will hang!

Proctor (*throws her down*). You mad, you murderous bitch!

Abigail. Oh, how hard it is when pretense falls! But it falls, it falls! (*She wraps herself up as though to go.*) You have done your duty by her. I hope it is your last hypocrisy. I pray you will come again with sweeter news for me. I know you will—now that your duty's done. Good night, John. (*She is backing* *away, raising her hand in farewell.*) Fear naught. I will save you tomorrow. (*As she turns and goes.*) From yourself I will save you. (*She is gone.* Proctor *is left alone, amazed, in terror. Takes up his lantern and slowly exits.*)

RELATED READINGS

Continued

Conversation with an American Writer

by Yevgeny Yevtushenko

translated from the Russian by George Reavey

Yevgeny Yevtushenko is a Russian poet who gained international fame in the 1960s for being outspoken despite the oppressive climate in the former Soviet Union. Like John Proctor, the speaker of this poem resists the pressure to denounce others and tries only to be honest.

"You have courage,"
                    they tell me.

It's not true.
                    I was never courageous.
I simply felt it unbecoming
to stoop to the cowardice of my colleagues.

5   I've shaken no foundations.
I simply mocked at pretense
                              and inflation.
Wrote articles.
                    Scribbled no denunciations.
And tried to speak all
                    on my mind.
Yes,
      I defended men of talent,

branding the hacks,
                              the would-be writers.
But this, in general, we should always do;
and yet they keep stressing my courage.
Oh, our descendants will burn with bitter
    shame
to remember, when punishing vile acts,
that most peculiar
                    time,
                              when
plain honesty
                    was labeled "courage" . . .

Guilt

by Clifford Lindsey Alderman

In a note preceding The Crucible, *Arthur Miller explains that in writing about the historical witch trials, he changed some of the characters. For example, he reduced the number of girls who made accusations. The following essay tells what happened to the actual participants in the Salem witch trials. One of those mentioned here, Ann Putnam, is the daughter of the character named Ann Putnam in the play.*

What happened in Salem Village had torn it asunder almost as surely as if a tornado had ripped and whirled through it.

It was split into two factions. On one side were those who had survived the terrible ordeal of arrest and imprisonment, their families, and the families of the men and women who had been executed. On the other were the people who had caused all this misery. A few months before, they had been the accusers, but now they were the accused.

As usual, when some great injustice is brought to light, no one wanted to take the blame. The guilty ones set about to find a scapegoat, thinking this would ease their own consciences.

Who but the Reverend Samuel Parris had caused this dishonor to fall upon Salem Village? The witchcraft delusion had begun right in his house. He had ferreted out the afflicted girls' secret of their sessions with Tituba. And he had relentlessly pursued his hunt for the witches he believed had tormented them. The congregation decided to drive him out.

In April, 1693, they passed a resolution stopping payment of Mr. Parris' salary. He was not one to submit tamely, however. He started a lawsuit, demanding payment.

The congregation struck back with a petition to the court. "Mr. Parris," it said, "has been the beginner and procurer of the sorest affliction, not to the village only, but to the whole country."

The lawsuit dragged on for several years, but this did not change the congregation's determination to be rid of its minister. Its leaders included not only those with guilty consciences, but the ones who had suffered most, especially the members of poor Rebecca Nurse's family. And most of Salem Village supported them.

Mr. Parris was hounded as he had hounded accused witches, but he hung on doggedly. At last he made one concession. He stood before his flock one Sabbath and read a kind of confession to them. It was called *Meditations of Peace*.

He admitted that the devil might take on the shape of persons who were innocent of any connection with him. "I beg, entreat and beseech you," he had written, "that Satan, the devil, the roaring lion, the old dragon, the enemy of all righteousness may no longer be served by us."

Then the minister offered his sympathy "to those who have suffered through the clouds of human weakness and Satan's wiles and sophistry." In a prayer he asked that God forgive him, and that all his flock "be covered with the mantle of love and we may forgive each other heartily, sincerely and thoroughly."

Whether the relatives and friends of those who had been hanged were comforted by his sympathy is not known, but they did not forgive him heartily. They went right on trying to drive him out.

At last, in 1695, the ministers of the villages north of Boston held a meeting in Salem Town to discuss what could be done to end the dispute. Mr. Parris finally agreed to go if his congregation would pay him £79, 9 shillings, sixpence he claimed they owed him. They decided it was well worth that sum to be rid of him. Then he and his family left Salem Village forever.

This was only one of the troubles that beset the village. For over a year it had been turned upside down by the witch hunt. Farmers and their wives had dropped everything to attend the examinations. The daily life of others had been disrupted when members of their families were jailed. Fields, gardens and livestock had been neglected. On many a farm in and around Salem Village, there was want.

But worst of all was the guilt. The stain of it could no more be rubbed out by the departure of Mr. Parris than could Lady Macbeth wash away the blood of the husband she had murdered. Her wail in Shakespeare's tragedy: "All the perfumes of Arabia will not sweeten this little hand," was true of many a hand in Salem Village.

What happened when the witchcraft delusion ended? How did it affect the afflicted girls? Did their torments instantly cease? How did they feel about the sudden collapse of the power and notoriety they had enjoyed? How did the rest of the people treat them? Was there any attempt to punish them?

For the most part, there is no answer to these questions. The histories of the village make no mention of the subject. Historians of the witchcraft delusion say nothing of it, save for what is known of the afflicted girls' later lives. Perhaps this is the strongest proof of the shame that Salem Village felt.

It wanted to forget, but it could not. For years it was torn by dissension. Families of those who had suffered did not speak to those of the accusers. People could not meet each other's gaze lest they see there a reflection of their own shame. Some moved away, among them Samuel and Mary Sibley (she had given Tituba the recipe for the "witch cake").

Public sentiment was now overwhelmingly against the whole witchcraft affair. There were demands that the colony's government take action to show the people's repentance. The General Court set aside January 15, 1697, as a day of atonement and fasting.

Guilt hung heavy upon many of those who had accused innocent persons or had had a part in sending them to be executed. No one knows how many repented, for undoubtedly some never confessed it.

Some did, however, though in most cases years passed before they spoke out. One of the first to do so was Samuel Sewall, though it took a tragedy in his own household to bring him to it.

Ever since he had sat on the Court of Oyer and Terminer, Judge Sewall's conscience had plagued him. He had helped to send nineteen persons to the gallows and Giles Cory to his frightful death. On December 23, 1696, his two-year-old daughter Sarah died. That next night, Christmas Eve, he sat sorrowing in his house on Beacon Hill in Boston.

He handed his Bible to his son Samuel. "Read to me, Sam," he said. "Mayhap I shall find consolation in the Word of God."

His son opened the book to the Gospel according to St. Matthew. The younger Samuel stumbled over the verses, for his father's Bible was in Latin.

Suddenly the judge stiffened and grew tense at the words, "But if ye had known what this meaneth: 'I will have mercy and not sacrifice,' ye would not have condemned the guiltless."

Ye would not have condemned the guiltless. The words struck the judge with terrible force. In his diary for that day he wrote, "Sam recites to me in Latin Matthew 12 from the 6th to the 12th verses. The 7th verse did awfully bring to mind the Salem Tragedie."

Perhaps he wondered whether the vengeful God of the Puritans had taken his child because he too had condemned the guiltless.

A few days later he went to his pastor, the same Samuel Willard who had worked to obtain fair trials for the accused witches.

"I can bear my guilt no longer," he told the minister. "I must make public confession of the wrong I have done by putting up a bill in the church. Will you read it to the congregation on the fast day?"

"Putting up a bill" was a common practice in colonial New England. It was an announcement posted in the church telling of some occasion of joy or sadness which had befallen a man, his family or his intimate friends.

On the fast day the General Court had proclaimed, Samuel Sewall stood humbly before the congregation of the Third Church while Mr. Willard read his confession. From then until the end of his long life, on the anniversary of the fast day, Judge Sewall did penance, the true and sincere repentance of a good man. Save for Nathaniel Saltonstall, who discovered his mistake so early, none of the other judges ever admitted they had been wrong.

In spite of his confession, guilt weighed upon Samuel Sewall's mind for years. As late as 1720 he read a passage in a history of New England about the witchcraft delusion, in which his name was mentioned among the judges. Referring to it, he wrote in his diary, "The good and gracious God be pleased to save New England and me and my family!"

Another confession was made on the fast day. It was a statement signed by Thomas Fisk, the foreman, and the other eleven members of the jury which had reversed its decision and convicted Rebecca Nurse.

"We fear we have been instrumental, with others, though ignorantly and unwittingly, to bring upon ourselves and this people of the Lord the guilt of innocent blood," it said. "We do heartily ask forgiveness of all whom we have offended."

Another man whose conscience would not let him alone was the Beverly minister, John Hale. He had shown Bridget Bishop no mercy when she was accused of killing the insane woman, Christina Trask, by witchcraft. When Goodwife Trask died, Mr. Hale had said she committed suicide. Yet before the Court of Oyer and Terminer he testified the woman had been murdered by supernatural means.

It was a different matter, however, when his own wife was cried out on. She was never arrested, but it made Mr. Hale do some serious thinking. Too many people were being accused. His wife was no witch. There must be others like her . . .

He was still not fully convinced, however. Then came Governor Phips' release of the accused persons who were in prison. Mr. Hale believed the loosing of such a great flock of witches would be a catastrophe. They would surely take revenge, tormenting scores of their accusers. Nothing of the sort happened.

Five years after the end of the witchcraft delusion, Mr. Hale could no longer struggle with his conscience. He wrote a pamphlet called *A Modest Inquiry into the Nature of Witchcraft,* which was published in 1698. In it he admitted he had made mistakes. He said there had been "a going too far in this affair." He added, "It cannot be imagined that in a place of such knowledge, so many in so small a compass of land, should so abominably leap into the Devil's lap at once."

Even Cotton Mather retreated. His sleep at night was disturbed by the fears of a guilty conscience. On November 15, 1696 he wrote in his diary, "Being afflicted last Night with discouraging Thoughts as if . . . the Divine Displeasure must overtake my Family for my not appearing with Vigor enough to stop the proceedings of the Judges when the Inextricable Storm from the Invisible World assaulted the Countrey, I did this morning, in prayer with my Family, putt my Family into the Merciful Hands of the Lord." He added that he had received assurance from the Lord that no vengeance would be taken against him or his family.

One more confession was yet to come. It was by one of the afflicted girls who had done the most, by her accusations and testimony, to send innocent people to Gallows Hill.

Ann Putnam's life, after the witchcraft delusion ended, was not an easy one. Her mother was sick of body as well as mind, and her health declined rapidly. In 1699, when Ann was nineteen, both her parents died within about two weeks of each other. There were younger children in the family, whose care fell upon Ann. The work was hard, she had never been strong, and her health too became poor.

She must have suffered intensely from the guilty knowledge of what she had done. At last, deeply troubled, she went to the Reverend Joseph Green, who had succeeded Mr. Parris as the minister in Salem Village.

"I do not know why I did those grievous things," she told him, "but I must confess my sin before all the people."

"You were very young then," Mr. Green said gently, "and you had fallen under Satan's power. But you are right in wishing to make confession that you were wrong. It will ease the burden upon your soul."

"Will you help me?" Ann pleaded. "I want to beg forgiveness of all I have wronged, especially Goodwife Nurse's family."

"We will draw up your confession and then discuss it with her son Samuel," said the minister.

There had been great bitterness between the Nurse family and Ann's. It would never be completely forgotten, but Samuel Nurse, after he had read the confession, agreed that it was suitable.

Not only the congregation of the Salem Village meetinghouse, but people from miles around filled every inch of space there on August 25, 1706. The silence when Mr. Green took his place in the pulpit was awesome. There must have been many who contrasted it with the riotous scenes which had taken place there during the examinations of accused witches in 1692.

No one breathed as Ann Putnam rose in her place on the women's side of the broad aisle. She stood with her head bowed.

Mr. Green began to read: "I desire to be humbled before God . . . that I, then being in my childhood, should . . . be made an instrument for the accusation of several persons of a grievous crime, whereby their lives were taken away from them. . . . I now have just grounds and good reason to believe they were innocent persons."

Ann's confession went on to say that what she had done was not due to anger, malice or ill will toward any persons. She said she had done so ignorantly, being deluded by Satan.

Then she concluded: "And particularly since I was a chief instrument of accusing Goodwife Nurse and her two sisters, I desire to lie in the dust and earnestly beg forgiveness of God and from all those unto whom I have given just cause of sorrow and offense, whose relations were taken away and accused."

As far as is known, Ann Putnam was the only one of the afflicted girls who confessed she was wrong or ever showed the slightest remorse for the grief and suffering she had caused.

The First Church in Salem Town also sought to make amends to Rebecca Nurse, who had been so cruelly excommunicated there before her execution. Twenty years later, on March 2, 1712, Rebecca's excommunication was revoked.

So was that of Giles Cory, who had been given the same treatment before he was pressed to death. But in Giles's case the church was not content simply to make atonement for the wrong which had been done him. The document which erased his excommunication stated this was done because he had bitterly repented his refusal to plead either guilty or innocent before the Court of Oyer and Terminer. There is no other record to show that the brave old man retreated an inch from his decision never to be tried for what he had not done.

Could anything else be done to compensate those who had either suffered themselves or had lost relatives? Many of those who had escaped the gallows, and the families of the ones who had not, were determined to have redress from the colony's government.

Philip English was their leader. His anger was hot, perhaps reasonably enough. He had not only lost a large sum in property which had been seized, but his wife Mary had died soon after they returned to Salem Town from their refuge in New York. Some accounts have it that her death was due to a lung ailment she contracted in the dampness and chill of Boston Prison.

English's rage was directed chiefly at Sheriff George Corwin, who had seized his property. He brought a suit for damages against Corwin in 1694, but the court decided that since the sheriff had only been carrying out official orders he was blameless.

English, still seething, bided his time. His chance for revenge came in 1697, when Corwin died. English rode to the sheriff's house, seized his body, galloped off and hid it. Then he demanded that the family pay him £60 and three shillings. There was a terrible scandal in Salem Town, but before he gave up Corwin's body so that it could be buried, English collected the money.

His hatred also fell upon the Reverend Nicholas Noyes of the First Church in Salem Town. Noyes never admitted that the witch hunts had been wrong, but Philip English publicly called him the murderer of Rebecca Nurse and John Procter. Not only did English never again set foot in Noyes' church, but he founded a new one, St. Peter's, in Salem Town.

He was bitter against John Hathorne too. This feud continued to the end of English's life. Then, as he lay on his deathbed, one of his family suggested that he might like to forgive his one-time friend before he died.

"All right," English growled, "but if I get well I'll be damned if I forgive him!"

In 1709 a group of twenty-one accused witches and the children of those who had died submitted a demand to the General Court that compensation be paid for their sufferings and their good names be completely cleared. Others followed their lead.

Most of the convicted witches had been sent quickly enough to the gallows, but when it came to paying for the damage that had been done, the wheels of justice turned slowly. At last, in 1711, the legislature appropriated £598 and twelve shillings and cleared the accused ones of guilt. Samuel Sewall was appointed head of a committee to distribute the money.

Although this amount would have to be multiplied at least twenty times to make it comparable to money values now, it was a pittance to divide among so many. Philip English alone had demanded £1500 for the devastation the sheriff had wrought upon his property.

Elizabeth Procter, who had been saved from death by Governor Phips' proclamation before her baby was born, received £150 to pay for the loss of her husband and her own sufferings. The large family of the "little black minister" of Casco Bay, George Burroughs, got £50. Sarah Good's brood of children, including poor little Dorcas, whose mind was affected by her ordeal in prison, were given £30.

Others got small amounts too, but Philip English received nothing. Probably, in his anger, he offended some of the committee. The Massachusetts Bay legislature finally agreed to pay £200 for all he had undergone, but by that time he was dead, leaving only his heirs to enjoy the money.

The witchcraft delusion will always be an outstanding event in American history, yet with the passing of many years, people did forget just how terrible it was. The memory was brought back to them with stunning force in the 1950s, however.

Arthur Miller, the eminent playwright, saw that what had happened in 1692 had tremendous dramatic possibilities. His play about it, *The Crucible*, was produced in 1953 and had a long run. It is still often presented in theatres throughout the country.

Audiences gasped at the sufferings of the accused persons, Tituba's black arts and the shocking behavior of the afflicted girls. Also at about this time, a television broadcast dramatized the trial of Ann Pudeator, who was hanged as a witch in Salem Town.

Perhaps *The Crucible* and the television production influenced the Massachusetts legislature to clear the good names of the accused persons and their descendants. On August 28, 1957, it passed a resolution stating that because of the Court of Oyer and Terminer's actions in 1692 "no disgrace attaches to the said descendants or any of them [the accused witches] by reason of such proceedings." The legislators were careful to protect themselves, however, against the possibility that descendants of the accused persons might sue for damages. The resolution stated that it did not include any right to take legal action against the state.

What happened to the chief actors in the tragedy of Salem Village after it ended? Most of them simply disappear from the historical records. Something is known of a few, however.

The Reverend Samuel Parris's later career reminds one of *A Christmas Carol,* by Charles Dickens. It will be remembered that in this famous story the ghosts of persons who had persecuted and cheated others during their lifetimes were doomed to wander the earth forever, trying vainly to help the poor and needy. Mr. Parris wandered too, but his rovings came to an end before his death.

After he was ousted from Salem Village, the minister went to a church in Newton, another of the villages surrounding Boston. From there he moved to Concord. Next, late in 1697, he began preaching at Stow. Since he was the minister in these three places during a period of only about two years, it suggests that either he was unhappy or his congregations were unhappy with him.

Later, Mr. Parris was the pastor of two other churches, first at Dunstable and finally at Sudbury, where he died in 1720. His wife had died at about the time he left Salem Village.

Little Betty Parris went with her father, of course, and so, probably, did Abigail Williams, since she had been adopted by the Parrises. The only other record of the family is that Betty married Benjamin Barnes of Concord in 1710, when she was about twenty-seven years old.

Almost nothing is known of Ann Putnam after her confession in 1706. But her health must have continued to be poor, for she died some ten years later at the age of about thirty-six.

What befell the other afflicted girls remains largely a mystery. It is said that two or three came to bad ends, while Elizabeth Booth and Mary Walcott married and presumably settled down. But how many remained in Salem Village and how they were treated by other villagers remains a blank. Again, the historians of the village seem to have been reluctant to write of the witchcraft delusion.

Only one man who did write about it tells what happened to Tituba. She was sent to prison in Boston, it will be recalled, after she had confessed to having dealings with Satan. But she was never tried. The only record of her later history is in the writings of Robert Calef, who was a man of mystery himself.

He says that Tituba, being penniless, could not meet the charges which had to be paid before she could be released. Calef claims she remained in prison for some time, and at last, being a slave, she was sold to a new owner for the amount that was due. Of this strange woman's later history and that of her husband John Indian, there is nothing.

More is known of William Stoughton, the merciless chief justice of the Court of Oyer and Terminer and the Superior Court of Adjudicature. His later life brought him one reward which some might say was greater than he deserved.

It happened because hot-tempered Sir William Phips found himself in trouble with his enemies in Massachusetts Bay. Two of them sent a petition to William and Mary, asking that Phips be removed as governor. He straightaway sailed for England to defend himself against the charges. While waiting for his trial to begin, he fell ill and died in 1695.

With that, Stoughton automatically became acting governor. He remained in this post with all the privileges and power of a regular governor until 1699, when a new royal governor was appointed.

There were those who thought there was something strange in the way the Reverend Nicholas Noyes of the First Church of Salem Town died some years after the delusion ended. It has already been told that just before Sarah Good was hanged on Gallows Hill, he shouted that she knew very well she was a witch. Sarah denied it, and then said, "If you take my life, God will give you blood to drink."

Mr. Noyes was a very fat man. Like some other persons who are greatly overweight, he seems to have suffered from high blood pressure, for he died of a burst blood vessel which caused him to bleed internally. Some saw in it the fulfillment of Sarah Good's curse.

These are the scanty details of what is known of the later years of the principal characters in the tragedy of 1692–93. There remains only one big question: Why? What really caused the witchcraft delusion to begin, why did it continue and spread, and why did it end so abruptly and so completely that never again was a "witch" executed in America?

How to Spot a Witch

by Adam Goodheart

The belief in witches existed for centuries before the trials at Salem. Over time, a considerable body of folklore developed about how to identify witches. A contemporary writer explains the most popular methods.

Perhaps the reason witch-hunting has gotten a bad name is that some practitioners used rather crude methods to separate the guilty from the innocent. The notorious judges of the Holy Roman Empire, for example, simply applied thumbscrews until the unfortunate suspects confessed. And during the English witch craze in the 1640s, the Rev. John Gaule recorded that "every old woman with a wrinkled face, a furr'd brow, a hairy lip, a gobber tooth, a squint eye, a squeaking voice, or a scolding tongue . . . is not only suspected, but pronounced for a witch." (Sexism was regrettably widespread among Gaule's colleagues, even though both men and women could be witches.) But more discriminating European witch hunters used far more refined techniques, as described in early lawbooks, manuals and court records.

1. Devil's Marks and Witches' Teats According to many witch-hunting guides, it is best to start your examination by shaving the suspect's body and examining it for devil's marks. These are the spots where Satan brands his followers to seal their pact with him. An English jurist in 1630 described them as "sometimes like a blew spot, or a red spot, like a Flea-biting." One problem: In the vermin-ridden 17th century, such blemishes were hardly uncommon. So the witch hunters devised an ingenious solution. The Devil, they reasoned, would not allow anything of his to be harmed. Therefore, they pricked any suspicious marks with a long silver pin. If the spot didn't bleed or was insensitive to pain, the suspect was a witch.

English experts believed witches often had extra nipples that they used to suckle demons. Matthew Hopkins, a witch hunter under Oliver Cromwell, exposed one woman as a witch when she was "found to have three teats about her, which honest women have not."

2. The Swimming Test If the hunt for teats and devil's marks proves inconclusive, you may have to resort to a popular folk method, the "swimming test." First, sprinkle the suspect with holy water. Tie his right thumb to his left big toe, and his left thumb to his right big toe. Fasten a rope around his waist. Then toss him into a pond or river. If he floats, he's a witch. If he sinks, haul him back in and set him free. The theoretical basis for this is simple, explained James VI of Scotland in 1597: "The water shall refuse to receive in her bosom those who have shaken off the sacred water of baptism."

Other popular tests include weighing the suspect against a very heavy Bible (if she weighs less than the book, she is guilty) and asking her to recite the Lord's Prayer without making a mistake. (In 1663, a defendant was convicted after repeatedly failing to do better than "Lead us into temptation" or "Lead us not into no temptation.") When you suspect a witch has murdered someone, ask her to lay her hands on the victim's body. If she is guilty, the corpse will start to bleed.

3. Nabbing the Elusive Imp One of the most devious ways to foil witches is to catch them with their familiars, the imps in animal form who do their nefarious bidding. Many witch hunters believed that the imps could not go for more than 24 hours without being suckled by their master or mistress. Therefore, when you have a suspect in prison, drill a peephole in the cell door and keep a close watch. If you see a rat, mouse or beetle in the cell, you've nabbed an imp. Beware of even the most improbable animals. In 1645, an Englishman named John Bysack confessed that for the last 20 years, he had regularly suckled imps in the form of snails.

4. Asking the Right Questions Even stubborn suspects will often collapse under skillful interrogation. Europe's most successful witch hunters were expert at framing questions of the when-did-you-stop-beating-your-wife sort. The justices of Colmar in Alsace used to lead off with "How long have you been a witch?" before moving on to more specific inquiries such as "What plagues of vermin and caterpillars have you created?"

WARNING:

According to the *Malleus Maleficarum (Hammer of Witches)*, a comprehensive witch-hunting guide published in 1486, judges at witchcraft trials should take precautions against being bewitched by the accused. Always wear protection: A wax medallion containing a bit of salt blessed on Palm Sunday, worn round the neck, will defend you from Satan's wiles. Otherwise, you yourself could end up on the wrong end of a witch hunt.

Young Goodman Brown

by Nathaniel Hawthorne

Descended from Judge Hathorne of the Salem witch trials, Nathaniel Hawthorne felt ashamed of his Puritan ancestors and often portrayed them unfavorably in his writing. In this story a young Puritan learns more about the devil's work than he wants to.

Young Goodman Brown came forth, at sunset, into the street of Salem village, but put his head back, after crossing the threshold, to exchange a parting kiss with his young wife. And Faith, as the wife was aptly named, thrust her own pretty head into the street, letting the wind play with the pink ribbons of her cap, while she called to Goodman Brown.

'Dearest heart,' whispered she, softly and rather sadly, when her lips were close to his ear, 'pr'y thee, put off your journey until sunrise, and sleep in your own bed to-night. A lone woman is troubled with such dreams and such thoughts, that she's afeard of herself, sometimes. Pray, tarry with me this night, dear husband, of all nights in the year!'

'My love and my Faith,' replied young Goodman Brown, 'of all nights in the year, this one night must I tarry away from thee. My journey, as thou callest it, forth and back again, must needs be done 'twixt now and sunrise. What, my sweet, pretty wife, dost thou doubt me already, and we but three months married!'

'Then, God bless you!' said Faith, with the pink ribbons, 'and may you find all well, when you come back.'

'Amen!' cried Goodman Brown. 'Say thy prayers, dear Faith, and go to bed at dusk, and no harm will come to thee.'

So they parted; and the young man pursued his way, until, being about to turn the corner by the meeting house, he looked back, and saw the head of Faith still peeping after him, with a melancholy air, in spite of her pink ribbons.

'Poor little Faith!' thought he, for his heart smote him. 'What a wretch am I, to leave her on such an errand! She talks of dreams, too. Methought, as she spoke, there was trouble in her face, as if a dream had warned her what work is to be done to-night. But, no, no! 'twould kill her to think it. Well; she's a blessed angel on earth; and after this one night, I'll cling to her skirts and follow her to Heaven.'

With this excellent resolve for the future, Goodman Brown felt himself justified in making more haste on his present evil purpose. He had taken a dreary road, darkened by all the gloomiest trees of the forest, which barely stood aside to let the narrow path creep through, and closed immediately behind. It was all as lonely as could be; and there is this peculiarity in such a solitude, that the traveller knows not who may be concealed by the innumerable trunks and the thick boughs overhead; so that, with lonely footsteps, he may yet be passing through an unseen multitude.

'There may be a devilish Indian behind every tree,' said Goodman Brown, to himself; and he glanced fearfully behind him, as he added, 'What if the devil himself should be at my very elbow!'

His head being turned back, he passed a crook of the road, and looking forward again, beheld the figure of a man, in grave and decent attire, seated at the foot of an old tree. He arose, at Goodman Brown's approach, and walked onward, side by side with him.

'You are late, Goodman Brown,' said he. 'The clock

of the Old South was striking as I came through Boston; and that is full fifteen minutes agone.'

'Faith kept me back awhile,' replied the young man, with a tremor in his voice, caused by the sudden appearance of his companion, though not wholly unexpected.

It was now deep dusk in the forest, and deepest in that part of it where these two were journeying. As nearly as could be discerned, the second traveller was about fifty years old, apparently in the same rank of life as Goodman Brown, and bearing a considerable resemblance to him, though perhaps more in expression than features. Still, they might have been taken for father and son. And yet, though the elder person was as simply clad as the younger, and as simple in manner too, he had an indescribable air of one who knew the world, and would not have felt abashed at the governor's dinner-table, or in King William's court, were it possible that his affairs should call him thither. But the only thing about him, that could be fixed upon as remarkable, was his staff, which bore the likeness of a great black snake, so curiously wrought, that it might almost be seen to twist and wriggle itself, like a living serpent. This, of course, must have been an ocular deception, assisted by the uncertain light.

'Come, Goodman Brown!' cried his fellow-traveller, 'this is a dull pace for the beginning of a journey. Take my staff, if you are so soon weary.'

'Friend,' said the other, exchanging his slow pace for a full stop, 'having kept covenant by meeting thee here, it is my purpose now to return whence I came. I have scruples, touching the matter thou wot'st of.'

'Sayest thou so?' replied he of the serpent, smiling apart. 'Let us walk on, nevertheless, reasoning as we go, and if I convince thee not, thou shalt turn back. We are but a little way in the forest, yet.'

'Too far, too far!' exclaimed the goodman, unconsciously resuming his walk. 'My father never went into the woods on such an errand, nor his father before him. We have been a race of honest men and good Christians, since the days of the martyrs. And shall I be the first of the name of Brown, that ever took this path, and kept—'

'Such company, thou wouldst say,' observed the elder person, interpreting his pause. 'Well said, Goodman Brown! I have been as well acquainted with your family as with ever a one among the Puritans; and that's no trifle to say. I helped your grandfather, the constable, when he lashed the Quaker woman so smartly through the streets of Salem. And it was I that brought your father a pitch-pine knot, kindled at my own hearth, to set fire to an Indian village, in King Philip's war. They were my good friends, both; and many a pleasant walk have we had along this path, and returned merrily after midnight. I would fain be friends with you, for their sake.'

'If it be as thou sayest,' replied Goodman Brown, 'I marvel they never spoke of these matters. Or, verily, I marvel not, seeing that the least rumor of the sort would have driven them from New-England. We are a people of prayer, and good works, to boot, and abide no such wickedness.'

'Wickedness or not,' said the traveller with the twisted staff, 'I have a very general acquaintance here in New-England. The deacons of many a church have drunk the communion wine with me; the selectmen, of divers towns, make me their chairman; and a majority of the Great and General Court are firm supporters of my interest. The governor and I, too—but these are state-secrets.'

'Can this be so!' cried Goodman Brown, with a stare of amazement at his undisturbed companion. 'Howbeit, I have nothing to do with the governor and council; they have their own ways, and are no rule for a simple husbandman, like me. But, were I to go on with thee, how should I meet the eye of that good old man, our minister, at Salem village? Oh, his voice would make me tremble, both Sabbath-day and lecture-day!'

Thus far, the elder traveller had listened with due gravity, but now burst into a fit of irrepressible mirth, shaking himself so violently, that his snake-like staff actually seemed to wriggle in sympathy.

'Ha! ha! ha!' shouted he, again and again; then composing himself, 'Well, go on, Goodman Brown, go on; but pr'y thee, don't kill me with laughing!'

'Well, then, to end the matter at once,' said Goodman Brown, considerably nettled, 'there is my wife, Faith. It would break her dear little heart; and I'd rather break my own!'

'Nay, if that be the case,' answered the other, 'e'en go thy ways, Goodman Brown. I would not, for twenty old women like the one hobbling before us, that Faith should come to any harm.'

As he spoke, he pointed his staff at a female figure on the path, in whom Goodman Brown recognized a very pious and exemplary dame, who had taught him his catechism, in youth, and was still his moral and spiritual adviser, jointly with the minister and Deacon Gookin.

'A marvel, truly, that Goody Cloyse should be so far in the wilderness, at night-fall!' said he. 'But, with your leave, friend, I shall take a cut through the woods, until we have left this Christian woman behind. Being a stranger to you, she might ask whom I was consorting with, and whither I was going.'

'Be it so,' said his fellow-traveller. 'Betake you to the woods, and let me keep the path.'

Accordingly, the young man turned aside, but took care to watch his companion, who advanced softly along the road, until he had come within a staff's length of the old dame. She, meanwhile, was making the best of her way, with singular speed for so aged a woman, and mumbling some indistinct words, a prayer, doubtless, as she went. The traveller put forth his staff, and touched her withered neck with what seemed the serpent's tail.

'The devil!' screamed the pious old lady.

'Then Goody Cloyse knows her old friend?' observed the traveller, confronting her, and leaning on his writhing stick.

'Ah, forsooth, and is it your worship, indeed?' cried the good dame. 'Yea, truly is it, and in the very image of my old gossip, Goodman Brown, the grandfather of the silly fellow that now is. But—would your worship believe it?—my broomstick hath strangely disappeared, stolen, as I suspect, by that unhanged witch, Goody Cory, and that, too, when I was all anointed with the juice of smallage and cinque-foil and wolf's-bane—'

'Mingled with fine wheat and the fat of a new-born babe,' said the shape of old Goodman Brown.

'Ah, your worship knows the receipt,' cried the old lady, cackling aloud. 'So, as I was saying, being all ready for the meeting, and no horse to ride on, I made up my mind to foot it; for they tell me, there is a nice young man to be taken into communion to-night. But now your good worship will lend me your arm, and we shall be there in a twinkling.'

'That can hardly be,' answered her friend. 'I may not spare you my arm, Goody Cloyse, but here is my staff, if you will.'

So saying, he threw it down at her feet, where, perhaps, it assumed life, being one of the rods which its owner had formerly lent to the Egyptian Magi. Of this fact, however, Goodman Brown could not take cognizance. He had cast up his eyes in astonishment, and looking down again, beheld neither Goody Cloyse nor the serpentine staff, but his fellow-traveller alone, who waited for him as calmly as if nothing had happened.

'That old woman taught me my catechism!' said the young man; and there was a world of meaning in this simple comment.

They continued to walk onward, while the elder traveller exhorted his companion to make good speed and persevere in the path, discoursing so aptly, that his arguments seemed rather to spring up in the bosom of his auditor, than to be suggested by himself. As they went, he plucked a branch of maple, to serve for a walking-stick, and began to strip it of the twigs and little boughs, which were wet with evening dew. The moment his fingers touched them, they became strangely withered and dried up, as with a week's sunshine. Thus the pair proceeded, at a good free pace, until suddenly, in a gloomy hollow of the road, Goodman Brown sat himself down on the stump of a tree, and refused to go any farther.

'Friend,' said he, stubbornly, 'my mind is made up. Not another step will I budge on this errand. What if a wretched old woman do choose to go to the devil, when I thought she was going to Heaven! Is that any reason why I should quit my dear Faith, and go after her?'

'You will think better of this, by-and-by,' said his acquaintance, composedly. 'Sit here and rest yourself awhile; and when you feel like moving again, there is my staff to help you along.'

Without more words, he threw his companion the maple stick, and was as speedily out of sight, as if he had vanished into the deepening gloom. The young man sat a few moments, by the road-side, applauding himself greatly, and thinking with how clear a conscience he should meet the minister, in his morning-walk, nor shrink from the eye of good old Deacon Gookin. And what calm sleep would be his, that very night, which was to have been spent so wickedly, but purely and sweetly now, in the arms of Faith! Amidst these pleasant and praiseworthy meditations, Goodman Brown heard the tramp of horses along the road, and deemed it advisable to conceal himself within the verge of the forest, conscious of the guilty purpose that had brought him thither, though now so happily turned from it.

On came the hoof-tramps and the voices of the riders, two grave old voices, conversing soberly as they drew near. These mingled sounds appeared to pass along the road, within a few yards of the young man's hiding-place; but owing, doubtless, to the depth of the gloom, at that particular spot, neither the travellers nor their steeds were visible. Though their figures brushed the small boughs by the way-side, it could not be seen that they intercepted, even for a moment, the faint gleam from the strip of bright sky, athwart which they must have passed. Goodman Brown alternately crouched and stood on tip-toe, pulling aside the branches, and thrusting forth his head as far as he durst, without discerning so much as a shadow. It vexed him the more, because he could have sworn, were such a thing possible, that he recognized the voices of the minister and Deacon Gookin, jogging along quietly, as they were wont to do, when bound to some ordination or ecclesiastical council. While yet within hearing, one of the riders stopped to pluck a switch.

'Of the two, reverend Sir,' said the voice like the deacon's, 'I had rather miss an ordination-dinner than to-night's meeting. They tell me that some of our community are to be here from Falmouth and beyond, and others from Connecticut and Rhode-Island; besides several of the Indian powwows, who, after their fashion, know almost as much deviltry as the best of us. Moreover, there is a goodly young woman to be taken into communion.'

'Mighty well, Deacon Gookin!' replied the solemn old tones of the minister. 'Spur up, or we shall be late. Nothing can be done, you know, until I get on the ground.'

The hoofs clattered again, and the voices, talking so strangely in the empty air, passed on through the forest, where no church had ever been gathered, nor solitary Christian prayed. Whither, then, could these holy men be journeying, so deep into the heathen wilderness? Young Goodman Brown caught hold of a tree, for support, being ready to sink down on the ground, faint and overburthened with the heavy sickness of his heart. He looked up to the sky, doubting whether there really was a Heaven above him. Yet, there was the blue arch, and the stars brightening in it.

'With Heaven above, and Faith below, I will yet stand firm against the devil!' cried Goodman Brown.

While he still gazed upward, into the deep arch of the firmament, and had lifted his hands to pray, a cloud, though no wind was stirring, hurried across the zenith, and hid the brightening stars. The blue sky was still visible, except directly overhead, where this black mass of cloud was sweeping swiftly northward. Aloft in the air, as if from the depths of the cloud, came a confused and doubtful sound of voices. Once, the listener fancied that he could distinguish the accents of town's-people of his own, men and women, both pious and ungodly, many of whom he had met at the communion-table, and had seen others rioting at the tavern. The next moment, so indistinct were the sounds, he doubted whether he had heard aught but the murmur of the old forest, whispering without a wind. Then came a stronger swell of those familiar tones, heard daily in the sunshine, at Salem village, but never, until now, from a cloud of night. There was one voice, of a young woman, uttering lamentations, yet with an uncertain sorrow, and entreating for some favor, which, perhaps, it would grieve her to obtain. And all the unseen multitude, both saints and sinners, seemed to encourage her onward.

'Faith!' shouted Goodman Brown, in a voice of agony and desperation; and the echoes of the forest mocked him, crying—'Faith! Faith!' as if bewildered wretches were seeking her, all through the wilderness.

The cry of grief, rage, and terror was yet piercing the night, when the unhappy husband held his breath for a response. There was a scream, drowned immediately in a louder murmur of voices, fading into far-off laughter, as the dark cloud swept away, leaving the clear and silent sky above Goodman Brown. But something fluttered lightly down through the air, and caught on the branch of a tree. The young man seized it, and beheld a pink ribbon.

'My Faith is gone!' cried he, after one stupefied moment. 'There is no good on earth; and sin is but a name. Come, devil! for to thee is this world given.'

And maddened with despair, so that he laughed loud and long, did Goodman Brown grasp his staff and set forth again, at such a rate, that he seemed to fly along the forest-path, rather than to walk or run. The road grew wilder and drearier, and more faintly traced, and vanished at length, leaving him in the heart of the dark wilderness, still rushing onward, with the instinct that guides mortal man to evil. The whole forest was peopled with frightful sounds; the creaking of the trees, the howling of wild beasts, and the yell of Indians; while, sometimes, the wind tolled like a distant church-bell, and sometimes gave a broad roar around the traveller, as if all Nature were laughing him to scorn. But he was himself the chief horror of the scene, and shrank not from its other horrors.

'Ha! ha! ha!' roared Goodman Brown, when the wind laughed at him. 'Let us hear which will laugh loudest! Think not to frighten me with your deviltry! Come witch, come wizard, come Indian powwow, come devil himself! and here comes Goodman Brown. You may as well fear him as he fear you!'

In truth, all through the haunted forest, there could be nothing more frightful than the figure of Goodman

Brown. On he flew, among the black pines, brandishing his staff with frenzied gestures, now giving vent to an inspiration of horrid blasphemy, and now shouting forth such laughter, as set all the echoes of the forest laughing like demons around him. The fiend in his own shape is less hideous, than when he rages in the breast of man. Thus sped the demoniac on his course, until, quivering among the trees, he saw a red light before him, as when the felled trunks and branches of a clearing have been set on fire, and throw up their lurid blaze against the sky, at the hour of midnight. He paused, in a lull of the tempest that had driven him onward, and heard the swell of what seemed a hymn, rolling solemnly from a distance, with the weight of many voices. He knew the tune; it was a familiar one in the choir of the village meeting-house. The verse died heavily away, and was lengthened by a chorus, not of human voices, but of all the sounds of the benighted wilderness, pealing in awful harmony together. Goodman Brown cried out; and his cry was lost to his own ear, by its unison with the cry of the desert.

In the interval of silence, he stole forward, until the light glared full upon his eyes. At one extremity of an open space, hemmed in by the dark wall of the forest, arose a rock, bearing some rude, natural resemblance either to an altar or a pulpit, and surrounded by four blazing pines, their tops aflame, their stems untouched, like candles at an evening meeting. The mass of foliage, that had overgrown the summit of the rock, was all on fire, blazing high into the night, and fitfully illuminating the whole field. Each pendent twig and leafy festoon was in a blaze. As the red light arose and fell, a numerous congregation alternately shone forth, then disappeared in shadow, and again grew, as it were, out of the darkness, peopling the heart of the solitary woods at once.

'A grave and dark-clad company!' quoth Goodman Brown.

In truth, they were such. Among them, quivering to-and-fro, between gloom and splendor, appeared faces that would be seen, next day, at the council-board of the province, and others which, Sabbath after Sabbath, looked devoutly heavenward, and benignantly over the crowded pews, from the holiest pulpits in the land. Some affirm, that the lady of the governor was there. At least, there were high dames well known to her, and wives of honored husbands, and widows, a great multitude, and ancient maidens, all of excellent repute, and fair young girls, who trembled, lest their mothers should espy them. Either the sudden gleams of light, flashing over the obscure field, bedazzled Goodman Brown, or he recognized a score of the church members of Salem village, famous for their especial sanctity. Good old Deacon Gookin had arrived, and waited at the skirts of that venerable saint, his revered pastor. But, irreverently consorting with these grave, reputable, and pious people, these elders of the church, these chaste dames and dewy virgins, there were men of dissolute lives and women of spotted fame, wretches given over to all mean and filthy vice, and suspected even of horrid crimes. It was strange to see, that the good shrank not from the wicked, nor were the sinners abashed by the saints. Scattered, also, among their pale-faced enemies, were the Indian priests, or powwows, who had often scared their native forest with more hideous incantations than any known to English witchcraft.

'But, where is Faith?' thought Goodman Brown: and, as hope came into his heart, he trembled.

Another verse of the hymn arose, a slow and mournful strain, such as the pious love, but joined to words which expressed all that our nature can conceive of sin, and darkly hinted at far more. Unfathomable to mere mortals is the lore of fiends. Verse after verse was sung, and still the chorus of the desert swelled between, like the deepest tone of a mighty organ. And, with the final peal of that dreadful anthem, there came a sound, as if the roaring wind, the rushing streams, the howling beasts, and every other voice of the unconverted wilderness were mingling and according with the voice of guilty man, in homage to the prince of all. The four blazing pines threw up a loftier flame, and obscurely discovered shapes and visages of horror on the smoke-wreaths, above the impious assembly. At the same moment, the fire on the rock shot redly forth, and formed a glowing arch above its base, where now appeared a figure. With reverence be it spoken, the figure bore no slight similitude, both in garb and manner, to some grave divine of the New-England churches.

'Bring forth the converts!' cried a voice, that echoed through the field and rolled into the forest.

At the word, Goodman Brown stept forth from the shadow of the trees, and approached the congregation, with whom he felt a loathful brotherhood, by the sympathy of all that was wicked in his heart. He could have well nigh sworn, that the shape of his own dead father beckoned him to advance, looking downward from a smoke-wreath, while a woman, with dim features of despair, threw out her hand to warn him back. Was it his mother? But he had no power to retreat one step, nor to resist, even in thought, when the minister and good old Deacon Gookin seized his arms, and led him to the blazing rock. Thither came also the slender form of a veiled female, led between Goody Cloyse, that pious teacher of the catechism, and Martha Carrier, who had received the devil's promise to be queen of hell. A rampant hag was she! And there stood the proselytes, beneath the canopy of fire.

'Welcome, my children,' said the dark figure, 'to the communion of your race! Ye have found, thus young, your nature and your destiny. My children, look behind you!'

They turned; and flashing forth, as it were, in a sheet of flame, the fiend-worshippers were seen: the smile of welcome gleamed darkly on every visage.

'There,' resumed the sable form, 'are all whom ye have reverenced from youth. Ye deemed them holier than yourselves, and shrank from your own sin, contrasting it with their lives of righteousness, and prayerful aspirations heavenward. Yet, here are they all, in my worshipping assembly! This night it shall be granted you to know their secret deeds; how hoary-bearded elders of the church have whispered wanton words to the young maids of their households; how many a woman, eager for widow's weeds, has given her husband a drink at bed-time, and let him sleep his last sleep in her bosom; how beardless youths have made haste to inherit their fathers' wealth; and how fair damsels—blush not, sweet ones!—have dug little graves in the garden, and bidden me, the sole guest, to an infant's funeral. By the sympathy of your human hearts for sin, ye shall scent out all the places—whether in church, bed-chamber, street, field, or forest—where crime has been committed, and shall exult to behold the whole earth one stain of guilt, one mighty bloodspot. Far more than this! It shall be yours to penetrate, in every bosom, the deep mystery of sin, the fountain of all wicked arts, and which inexhaustibly supplies more evil impulses than human power—than my power, at its utmost!—can make manifest in deeds. And now, my children, look upon each other.'

They did so; and, by the blaze of the hell-kindled torches, the wretched man beheld his Faith, and the wife her husband, trembling before that unhallowed altar.

'Lo! there ye stand, my children,' said the figure, in a deep and solemn tone, almost sad, with its despairing awfulness, as if his once angelic nature could yet mourn for our miserable race. 'Depending upon one another's hearts, ye had still hoped, that virtue were not all a dream. Now are ye undeceived! Evil is the nature of mankind. Evil must be your only happiness. Welcome, again, my children, to the communion of your race!'

'Welcome!' repeated the fiend-worshippers, in one cry of despair and triumph.

And there they stood, the only pair, as it seemed, who were yet hesitating on the verge of wickedness, in this dark world. A basin was hollowed, naturally, in the rock. Did it contain water, reddened by the lurid light? or was it blood? or, perchance, a liquid flame? Herein did the Shape of Evil dip his hand, and prepare to lay the mark of baptism upon their foreheads, that they might be partakers of the mystery of sin, more conscious of the secret guilt of others, both in deed and thought, than they could now be of their own. The husband cast one look at his pale wife, and Faith at him. What polluted wretches would the next glance shew them to each other, shuddering alike at what they disclosed and what they saw!

'Faith! Faith!' cried the husband. 'Look up to Heaven, and resist the Wicked One!'

Whether Faith obeyed, he knew not. Hardly had he spoken, when he found himself amid calm night and solitude, listening to a roar of the wind, which died heavily away through the forest. He staggered against the rock and felt it chill and damp, while a hanging twig, that had been all on fire, besprinkled his cheek with the coldest dew.

The next morning, young Goodman Brown came slowly into the street of Salem village, staring around him like a bewildered man. The good old minister was taking a walk along the grave-yard, to get an appetite for breakfast and meditate his sermon, and bestowed a blessing, as he passed, on Goodman Brown. He shrank from the venerable saint, as if to avoid an anathema. Old Deacon Gookin was at domestic worship, and the holy words of his prayer were heard through the open window. 'What God doth the wizard pray to?' quoth Goodman Brown. Goody Cloyse, that excellent old Christian, stood in the early sunshine, at her own lattice, catechising a little girl, who had brought her a pint of morning's milk. Goodman Brown snatched away the child, as from the grasp of the fiend himself. Turning the corner by the meeting-house, he spied the head of Faith, with the pink ribbons, gazing anxiously forth, and bursting into such joy at sight of him, that she skipt along the street, and almost kissed her husband before the whole village. But, Goodman Brown looked sternly and sadly into her face, and passed on without a greeting.

Had Goodman Brown fallen asleep in the forest, and only dreamed a wild dream of a witch-meeting?

Be it so, if you will. But, alas! it was a dream of evil omen for young Goodman Brown. A stern, a sad, a darkly meditative, a distrustful, if not a desperate man, did he become, from the night of that fearful dream. On the Sabbath-day, when the congregation were singing a holy psalm, he could not listen, because an anthem of sin rushed loudly upon his ear, and drowned all the blessed strain. When the minister spoke from the pulpit, with power and fervid eloquence, and, with his hand on the open Bible, of the sacred truths of our religion, and of saint-like lives and triumphant deaths, and of future bliss or misery unutterable, then did Goodman Brown turn pale, dreading, lest the roof should thunder down upon the gray blasphemer and his hearers. Often, awakening suddenly at midnight, he shrank from the bosom of Faith, and at morning or eventide, when the family knelt down at prayer, he scowled, and muttered to himself, and gazed sternly at his wife, and turned away. And when he had lived long, and was borne to his grave, a hoary corpse, followed by Faith, an aged woman, and children and grandchildren, a goodly procession, besides neighbors, not a few, they carved no hopeful verse upon his tomb-stone; for his dying hour was gloom.

The Great Fear

by J. Ronald Oakley

During the 1950s, Senator Joseph McCarthy and others led a campaign to make sure that there were no Communists in government or in any other positions of influence in the United States. This period of terror and persecution has been compared to the witch-hunt of the 1690s. However, instead of the dozens of people hurt by the witch trials, thousands of people had their lives ruined during the "Red" scare.

The atmosphere of fear and suspicion settling over the land in 1950 was skillfully exploited by many men, but none was more adept at the politics of fear than Senator Joseph R. McCarthy of Wisconsin, who in the first few months of the year would rise from obscurity to become one of the most admired, hated, and powerful men in America.

When the year began, few people in America knew much about the senator. Born in 1908 in Wisconsin to poor Irish-American parents, he was a graduate of Marquette University, a former circuit judge, and a former marine who was elected to the Senate in 1946 after using smear tactics to defeat veteran Senator Robert M. La Follette, Jr., in the primary election and Democrat Howard McMurray in the general election. His first three years in the Senate were undistinguished. Although a junior senator, he refused to follow Senate rules and customs, specialized in malicious attacks on his colleagues, and frequently thwarted committee work by trying to inject trivial and extraneous matters into committee discussions. A lazy and ineffectual senator, he was an easy captive for any lobbyist willing to put a few extra bucks into his personal or political bank accounts. He fought so vigorously and effectively for the sugar and soft drink industries that he became known around Washington as the Pepsi Cola Kid, and his shameless efforts for the real estate industry earned him the nickname Water Boy of the Real Estate Lobby. But none of these activities had brought him the fame and power he so desperately sought, and early in 1950 he was anxiously looking for some issue to enhance his reputation and guarantee his reelection in 1952.

Then, at a dinner meeting at the Colony Restaurant in Washington on January 7, an acquaintance suggested that the communists-in-government issue would attract national publicity and enhance his chances for reelection. Like other conservative Republican senators, McCarthy had occasionally raised this issue before in his speeches, but he now saw that in the charged political atmosphere of the new year, it could become the salvation of his fading political career. "That's it," he told his companions. "The government is full of Communists. We can hammer away at them." McCarthy left the dinner party excited about his new issue, and his ruthless exploitation of it would catapult him to national fame and, eventually, to disgrace.

Having "discovered" the communists-in-government issue, McCarthy asked the Senate Republican Campaign Committee to schedule several speaking engagements for him around the time of Lincoln's birthday. The committee obliged, and on February 9, McCarthy found himself speaking before the Ohio County Women's Republican Club in Wheeling, West Virginia. This was not quite the forum McCarthy had wanted, but he made the best of it. In a rambling, largely extemporaneous speech, he told the good Republican ladies gathered there that the United States had been the strongest nation in the world at the end of World War

II but had since fallen from that pinnacle of power through the incompetence and treason of men high in the government, particularly in the State Department. Then, waving a sheaf of paper, he said that "I have here in my hand a list of 205—a list of names that were made known to the Secretary of State as being members of the Communist Party and who nevertheless are still working and shaping policy in the State Department." The audience was stunned, and so was the rest of the nation when it read of these accusations on the front pages of the newspapers. McCarthy had found the issue he had been looking for.

McCarthy's Wheeling speech came at just the right time for maximum exposure and impact. Just a few months before, Russia had acquired the atomic bomb. Just a few weeks before, China had been "lost." Just three weeks before Hiss had been convicted of perjury. Just ten days before Truman had decided to build the H-bomb. And just six days before, Fuchs had confessed. McCarthy was as surprised as anyone at the national reaction to the Wheeling speech, but he quickly and skillfully capitalized on the issue. He could not remember what figure he had quoted at Wheeling—whether it was 205 or 209 or 57 or whatever—and his staff tried in vain to find someone who had recorded the speech so as to pinpoint the exact figure. But it did not matter to McCarthy. In Denver on February 10 he spoke of 205 "security risks," but in Salt Lake City the next day he transformed them into "57 card-carrying Communists," and in subsequent speeches the number of people involved and the nature of their crime continued to vary widely. By February 20, when he kept the Senate in session from late afternoon to around midnight with a rambling six-hour performance that embarrassed and outraged some senators, caused others to doze, and sent still others heading for the nearest exit, McCarthy was repudiating all his previous figures, talking about "81 cases," and bragging that he had penetrated "Truman's iron curtain of secrecy."

Hoping to restore confidence in the Truman administration by disproving McCarthy's allegations, the Senate Foreign Relations Committee established a subcommittee headed by Democratic Senator Millard E. Tydings of Maryland to investigate McCarthy's charges. The Tydings Committee began its hearings on March 8, and finally on July 14, after bitter partisan infighting aggravated by the trauma surrounding the outbreak of the Korean War, it issued a majority report dismissing all of McCarthy's allegations and condemning them as "a fraud and a hoax perpetrated on the Senate of the United States and the American people." However, Republican members of the subcommittee and of the Senate Foreign Relations Committee condemned the majority report and the Democrats who had signed it. Senator William E. Jenner accused Tydings of chairing "the most scandalous and brazen whitewash of treasonable conspiracy in our history." As for McCarthy, he showed his ability to turn defeat into victory through the great publicity he received and through his charges that the report was "a green light to the Red fifth column in the United States" as well as "a signal to the traitors, Communists, and fellow travelers in our Government that they need have no fear of exposure." In contrast to the Truman administration, which found itself in a no-win situation with the communists-in-government issue, McCarthy was, at least for the time being, in a no-lose situation. Many people were willing to believe his charges without any evidence or in the face of contrary evidence, and he profited from every bit of publicity—good or bad—that came his way.

Joe McCarthy was now one of the most famous men in America. He had made the front covers of

Time and *Newsweek* and many other magazines, and pictures of him and accounts of his Red-hunting activities appeared almost daily on the front pages of the newspapers. He was one of the most sought-after public speakers in the land, he was constantly pursued by reporters and photographers and autograph-seekers, he was widely touted as one of the most eligible bachelors in Washington, and his office was inundated with mail, mostly favorable, and often containing donations that totaled close to $1,000 a day. A Gallup poll on May 21 showed that 84 percent of the American people had heard of his charges against the State Department and that 39 percent of those who had heard of them felt that they were a good thing for the country. The outbreak of the Korean War on June 25 would force the senator to share the headlines with events from that far-off land, but it also added fuel to his charges and gave him a new issue to use against the Truman administration, which he could blame for encouraging the North Korean attack and for mis-handling the conduct of the war that was killing so many American boys. World events seemed to be playing into McCarthy's hands.

McCarthy would be in the spotlight for the next four years, gaining a power and influence usually beyond the reach of most senators and demagogues. He was a tireless campaigner for right-wing Republican candidates and was credited—probably erroneously—with securing the election of anywhere from six to twelve congressmen. He constantly harassed the Truman administration with his wild charges of incompetence and treason, with his brutal attacks on the State Department for losing China and giving Eastern Europe and the bomb to the Russians, with his attempts to block the president's nominees to State Department posts, and with his allegations of government bungling and treason in the conduct of the Korean war.

As McCarthy's fame grew, he became more vituperative and reckless, and instead of hinting at nameless "lists" and changing numbers of "communists in government," he began to name names—speaking always from the Senate floor, of course, so he could not be sued for libel. He branched out to attack and intimidate not just government officials but journalists, professors, and many other private citizens. He successfully resisted all attempts by the Senate and his own party to restrain him, cleverly manipulated the media, and gained even more power when the Republican victories of 1952 enabled him to assume the chairmanship of the Senate Committee on Government Operations and of that committee's Permanent Subcommittee on Investigations. In these positions he would overreach himself and bring about his own dramatic fall from power, but until then he basked in the publicity showered upon him by his supporters and critics, relished the myths of his political invincibility, and enjoyed the turmoil he was creating. . . .

McCarthy carried his lies to the floor and committee rooms of the Senate and to news conference and public events that were reported to audiences running into the millions. Most men would shrink from telling obvious lies under such public scrutiny, but not McCarthy. He lied about the backgrounds of his opponents, distorted their statements, and assassinated their characters with wild allegations. One of his favorite techniques was to pull a stack of papers from his old briefcase and, claiming that he held the evidence in his hand, taken from his files, to read from imaginary documents about imaginary people and imaginary events, making up names and numbers and events as he went along. Sometimes the "documents" were worthless sheets of paper, old government reports, or copies of legislation being deliberated by the Senate. It did not matter to McCarthy, who skillfully paraphrased and lied as he went along and warmed to his topic and audience. He denied requests to see the documents by claiming that they were secret documents given to him by his network of informants, parried requests for clarification by claiming that it was not his fault that the inquiring senator was too stupid to understand what he was saying, and evaded attempts to pin him down on his inconsistencies in the number of communists he had found by claiming that he was tired of this silly numbers game and wanted to get on to the heart of the matter. When backed into a corner and confronted with an obvious lie, he responded by attacking his adversary or dropping that line of investigation and going on to another. He would attack any person or organization as long as he got good publicity from it or until he ran into strong opposition; then he would drop that cause and pick up another.

McCarthy was a master at using inflammatory rhetoric that obscured his lack of facts, stuck in the minds of his listeners, and made newspaper headlines. For four years Americans were accustomed to hearing McCarthy lambast "left-wing bleeding hearts," "egg-sucking phony liberals," "Communists and queers who sold China into atheistic slavery," and "Parlor Pinks and Parlor Punks." He frequently talked of the "Yalta betrayal," the "sellout of China," and a State Department that was full of homosexuals and traitors "more loyal to the ideals and designs of Communism than to those of the free, God-fearing half of the world." He called Owen Lattimore (a Far Eastern expert and former part-time State Department consultant) "the top Russian espionage agent" in the United States, and the "principal architect of our far-eastern policy" that had led to the communist takeover of China. He habitually referred to Truman and Acheson as the "pied pipers of the Politburo," called Truman a "son of a bitch" after he fired General MacArthur, called

Acheson the Red Dean and the Red Dean of Fashion, and characterized General George C. Marshall, the highly revered army chief of staff during World War II and the secretary of state and then secretary of defense under Truman, as "a man steeped in falsehood" who was part "of a great conspiracy, a conspiracy on a scale so immense as to dwarf any previous such venture in the history of man." He said that Senator Ralph Flanders of Vermont was "senile" and that "they should get a man with a net and take him to a quiet place," and he described Senator Robert C. Hendrickson of New Jersey as "a living miracle in that he is without question the only man in the world who has lived so long with neither brains nor guts."

These malicious attacks went on and on for four years, as did his pledge to continue his battle against communism "regardless of how high-pitched becomes the squealing and screaming of those left-wing, bleeding heart, phony liberals." He was a ruthless, clever wordsmith. No wonder he became known as Low-Blow Joe, or that Joseph and Steward Alsop could write that "McCarthy is the only major politician in the country who can be labeled 'liar' without fear of libel," or that President Truman, when accused by Senator Robert A. Taft of libeling McCarthy, would ask a reporter, "Do you think that is possible?"

McCarthy was as dishonest in his financial affairs as he was in his rhetoric and his "investigations" and "exposés" of communists and other traitors. As Senate investigations later revealed, he received thousands of dollars in cash or unsecured loans from lobbyists in return for his vote on crucial issues. A large amount of the donations he received for his "fight for America" crusade went not into the fight against communism but into his personal checking account, where it was used to pay off gambling debts, to play the stock market, and buy soybean futures. He also violated several federal and state laws and regulations in the area of bribery, taxes, banking, and commodity trading.

What were the motives of this incredibly unscrupulous man? Many of his contemporary opponents compared him to Hitler and saw him as the leader of a right-wing totalitarian movement that was using the communist issue to establish a totalitarian state. McCarthy was like Hitler in his ruthlessness, his complete disregard for the truth, and his shrewd manipulation of the fears of the people. But here the comparison stops. Hitler was the leader of an ideological movement designed to take over the state and run it along totalitarian principles. McCarthy, however, had no social or economic program and did not seek control of the military or the government. He was not a fanatic or a fascist, and he never tried to organize or lead any movement. As historian Richard Hofstadter later wrote in his *The Paranoid Style in American Politics,* the slovenly senator "could barely organize his own files, much less a movement."

What McCarthy sought was publicity, fame, and reelection to the Senate. He loved to manipulate people, to create turmoil and confusion, to be able to swagger into a room and command the attention of everyone there, to see his name and picture in the paper. There is little evidence that he ever believed his own lies, that he ever really thought that communism was boring from within to destroy the American republic. Everything he did and said was calculated to bring maximum publicity and the fame he thirsted for. His wild charges, his tantrums, his staged walkouts from committee hearings, his badgerings of witnesses, his taunts, his sneers, his roughhouse language—all were shrewdly calculated to put him at the center of attention and gather headlines and votes. Communism in government was a convenient tool for him to use to further his own glory-seeking. Had the circumstances been different, he could just as easily have ridden the fears of a fascist, Jewish, or black "menace" to the top of the glory pole. He was a man without principles, scruples, beliefs, or proof of his sensational allegations. He never uncovered a single communist in the government, yet he had the support of millions. . . .

McCarthy was the most famous of the witchhunters, but he was certainly not the only one, for throughout the country many individuals, organizations, and government agencies were working for the same hysterical cause. It began at the top, with the federal government. From 1947 until 1954, when the hysteria began to decline, federal employees under both the Truman and Eisenhower administrations were subjected to a series of executive orders, laws of Congress, and Supreme Court rulings on loyalty and security regulations. During this period federal employees were investigated, prosecuted, and dismissed for a wide range of activities, including subversion, espionage, sabotage, belonging to the Communist party or some other totalitarian organization, "furthering" the interests of a foreign power, having "questionable" loyalty to the United States, taking the Fifth Amendment during loyalty hearings or trials, being a "security risk" in a "sensitive" job, having "dangerous" associations, and for a variety of activities that were believed (whether true or not) to lay federal employees open to blackmail, such as homosexuality, sexual promiscuity, and immoral conduct of various kinds.

The loyalty issue put the whole federal service under a cloud of suspicion and subjected thousands of employees to investigations by the loyalty boards within their departments, by the Justice Department, by the FBI, HUAC, and other government agencies. "An ugly, sinister, and completely stupid process of intimidation is undermining the morale of completely loyal government workers," wrote A. Powell Davies in *The New Republic* in early 1952. Federal employees were afraid to speak out on controversial topics, join organizations that might be tainted with the slightest suspicion of radicalism, subscribe to unusual periodicals, or associate with "suspicious" people. Employees under investigation quickly learned that they would be subjected to a whole range of questions and checks on their private beliefs and habits, such as what books do you read? Do you believe in God? Do you ever entertain black people in your home? Do you have any of Paul Robeson's records in your home? Do you believe that blood from white and black donors should be segregated in blood banks? In one silly incident, a Negro bootblack in the Pentagon was interviewed seventy times by the FBI before it finally decided that he was not a security risk and should be allowed to continue shining shoes there. The cause of this expensive and time-consuming investigation was the bootblack's $10 donation years before to a defense fund for the Scottsboro boys.

The results of the loyalty and security programs and investigations certainly never justified the cost in dollars, man hours, or damages to the reputations and careers of innocent people. Thousands of people were investigated, but under Truman only 1,210 were dismissed and another 6,000 resigned rather than submit to the indignities and publicity of a hearing or trial. During Eisenhower's first administration, around 1,500 were dismissed, while another 6,000 resigned. The Truman and Eisenhower administrations also deported 163 alien "subversives," far fewer than the 900 deported during the Red Scare of 1919–1920. In neither administration did the investigations turn up a genuine spy or saboteur—the dismissals were for being a "security risk" or for engaging in some form of "misconduct," such as alcoholism, adultery, or homosexuality. Many of those who resigned were valuable federal employees. The State Department was especially hard hit by the resignations, losing many of its foreign policy experts, especially those in the area of Far Eastern Affairs, who fell under the most suspicion because of the "loss" of China.

It was not just government employees who suffered. HUAC reached out to investigate and ruin the reputations of private citizens from all walks of life, and in December of 1950 the Senate, fearful of being left out in the crusade against communism, established its own version of HUAC, the Internal Security Subcommittee of the Committee of the Judiciary. And just a few months before, in September, the Senate and the House had joined to pass over Truman's veto the most restrictive of all the internal security measures, the McCarran Internal Security Act. Named for its major sponsor, Democratic Senator Pat McCarran of Nevada, this act required all communist organizations and communist-front organizations to register with the attorney general's office, banned communists from working in defense plants, prohibited government employees from contributing money to any communist organization or from being a member of any organization conspiring to set up a totalitarian state in the United States, and gave the government the power to halt the immigration of subversive aliens and to deport those already in this country. The bill also gave the president the power to declare a national security emergency, during which the government could arrest and detain in special concentration camps anyone suspected of conspiracy, espionage, or sabotage until they had been given a hearing before a Detention Review Board. No one was ever put in these camps, but many critics found it astonishing that they were established in a country claiming to be the freest nation in the world and to be the free world's leader in the battle against international communism.

During the Great Fear the states followed the example of the federal government and joined in the anticommunist crusade. By the time Eisenhower took office in 1953, thirty-nine states had passed laws making it a criminal offense to advocate the violent overthrow of the government or join any organization advocating the violent overthrow of the government, twenty-six had passed laws prohibiting communists from running for public office, twenty-eight had closed civil service ranks to communists, thirty-two had enacted loyalty oaths for teachers, and most states had outlawed the Communist party. A Connecticut sedition law made it illegal to criticize the United States government, the army, or the American flag, while Texas made membership in the Communist party a felony punishable by twenty years' imprisonment. In many states laws were passed making the taking of the Fifth Amendment automatic proof of Communist party membership and automatic grounds for summary dismissal from government service. And at the local level, in municipal and county governments, authorities often tried to rival the state and federal government in the zeal with which they enacted antisubversive laws and regulations. Many towns passed their own loyalty oaths for public employees and ordered communists to register with the police, or simply ordered them to get out of town.

It was virtually impossible in this atmosphere for accused communists to get a fair trial. The most publicized example of this was the fate of Julius and Ethel Rosenberg, arrested in 1950 for allegedly passing atomic secrets to the Russians. The trial of the Rosenbergs and several of their codefendents for violation of the Espionage Act of 1917 began on March 6, 1951, at the federal courthouse at Foley Square in New York, during some of the darkest days of the Korean War. During the two-week trial Ethel's brother and sister-in-law, David and Ruth Greenglass, testified that the Rosenbergs had recruited them as accomplices in a vast conspiracy to transmit secrets of the atomic bomb to Russia during the Second World War, when Julius had worked as a civilian engineer in the Brooklyn supply office of the Army Signal Corps before being dismissed by the army in March of 1945 on the grounds that he was a communist. According to the Greenglasses, the Rosenbergs were motivated by the belief that, if both Russia and America had the bomb, it would never be used, and world peace would be assured. The Rosenbergs denied all allegations, claimed that they had been framed by the government, and took the Fifth Amendment when asked if they were or had ever been communists. They steadfastly argued that they were the victims of American fascism, anti-Semitism, and the anticommunist hysteria of the time.

But the jury believed otherwise, and on March 29 it pronounced the Rosenbergs guilty of a conspiracy to commit espionage. On April 15, Judge Irving Kaufman sentenced the Rosenbergs to die in the electric chair. Their crime, he told the court, was "worse than murder," because it had helped the Russians acquire the atomic bomb much earlier than they would have otherwise, had encouraged communist aggression in Korea, and furthered the goal of world communism. "It is not in my power, Julius and Ethel Rosenberg, to forgive you," he said. "Only the Lord can find mercy for what you have done." The Rosenbergs' coconspirators were convicted of lesser degrees of conspiracy and given lighter sentences, ranging from fifteen to thirty years.

All across the country people kept up with the Rosenberg trial, read their published letters, followed the newspaper stories of their two little sons' visits with their parents at Sing Sing prison, and debated their guilt and their death sentence. Many felt that the

Rosenbergs were guilty and deserved their fate, others accepted their guilt but believed that the punishment was too harsh, others believed that they were probably guilty but had not received a fair trial in Judge Irving Kaufman's court, and some felt that they were innocent victims of the anticommunist hysteria of the time and of a long-standing willingness by some to believe in an international Jewish conspiracy. Many were disturbed by the fact that the Rosenbergs were tried and convicted by the press long before they entered the courtroom, that most of the testimony against them came from confessed spies trying to reduce their sentence by turning witnesses for the prosecution, and that they were convicted of conspiring to pass secrets to Russia at a time when Russia was an ally of the United States, not an enemy. At home and abroad, the case was frequently compared to the Sacco and Vanzetti case of the twenties in America and to the Dreyfus case in France in the latter part of the nineteenth century. It would be a big headline-getter until the couple's execution in the early months of the Eisenhower administration.

One of the major victims of the Great Fear was the movie industry, a natural target since it dealt with the dissemination of ideas to a mass audience. From the mid-1930s to the mid-1950s perhaps as many as 300 Hollywood writers, directors, actors, set designers, and others connected with the movie industry had joined the Communist party, which always drew a large percentage of its membership from the intellectual and artistic class in America. But few if any communist ideas ever got into Hollywood's movies, for the conservative business interests that financed the making of movies shied away from supporting films with controversial themes, much less communist ones. No film was ever proved to be communist in origin or content in spite of all the publicity surrounding the "communists in Hollywood" controversy. But this didn't stop HUAC and other superpatriotic organizations from wreaking havoc on the industry.

The Great Fear began in Hollywood in 1947 when HUAC began a series of investigations and hearings on communist infiltration of the movie industry. Many people in Hollywood quickly caved in to HUAC and the Great Fear. Some appeared before HUAC and named names of colleagues who were communists or suspected communists or who had tried to recruit them for the cause. Blacklists were quickly circulated of communists or suspected communists or anyone else who did anything to arouse the kind of suspicion that might cause unwanted publicity and controversy for forthcoming pictures. According to some estimates, perhaps as many as 500 people—writers, directors, actors and actresses, and others associated with the making of films—found their name on the blacklists. Among the prominent names on the list could be found those of actors Will Geer and Jeff Corey, pantomime Zero Mostel, and writers Lillian Hellman, Ring Lardner, Jr., and Arthur Miller. Some were never able to work again, while others, like Will Geer, could find little or no work for over a decade—and often it was too late by then to resume an aborted career.

In addition to the infamous blacklists, Hollywood also reacted to the Great Fear by severely reducing the number of films dealing with serious social issues and controversial subjects and replacing them with escapist entertainment—westerns, cops and robbers, comedies, and musicals. And to show just how patriotic it was, Hollywood turned out more and more war films and anticommunist films. About forty anticommunist films were made, with titles like *I Was a Communist for the FBI, The Steel Fist, and The Red Menace*. Perhaps the best example of this genre was *My Son John* (1952), a morality tale about a nice, small-town boy who went off to college and was duped into becoming a pacifist, an atheist, and perhaps even a homosexual and communist by his intellectual professors and liberal friends, and was then assassinated gangland style on the steps of the Lincoln Memorial after his corrupters discovered that he had repented of his errors and was going to the FBI with his confession. The effect that the suspicion was having on Hollywood can be also seen in the decision by Monogram Pictures in 1950 to cancel plans for a movie on Hiawatha because, according to studio executives, Hiawatha's attempts to arrange peace with the Indians "might be regarded as a message of peace and therefore helpful to Russian designs."

Like the movies, the radio and television industry was a natural target of the anticommunist hysteria, because it dealt with a wide variety of ideas and broadcast to a mass audience. The industry was under attack from 1947 onward, but the major blow came in 1950 with the publication of *Red Channels: The Report of Communist Influence in Radio and Television,* written by former FBI agents Kenneth M. Bierly, John G. Keenan, and Theodore C. Kirkpatrick. Fear of lawsuits prevented the authors from claiming that any of the people listed inside the book were communists, but it contained an alphabetical list of 151 prominent people in the radio and television industry along with a "citation" of each individual's activities on behalf of various causes. These "citations" gave the unmistakable impression that these individuals had belonged to organizations and participated in activities that aided the communist cause. And what were they accused of, or "cited" for, in this literary smear? They were cited for fighting race discrimination, combatting censorship, criticizing HUAC, opposing Hitler and other fascists in the thirties and forties, advocating better Russian-American relations, favoring New Deal legislation, signing petitions for "liberal" or "pacifist" causes, supporting the United Nations, and campaigning for Henry Wallace. Among those cited for these so-called subversive activities were Lee J. Cobb, Leonard Bernstein, Aaron Copland, Jose Ferrer, Will Geer, Gypsy Rose Lee, Burgess Meredith, Edward G. Robinson, and Orson Welles.

Published on June 22, just three days before the outbreak of the Korean War, copies of *Red Channels* soon found their way to the desks of radio and television executives and sponsors, who in the hysterical climate of 1950 wanted no connection with controversial ideas or controversial individuals. Without being given the opportunity to defend themselves against the charges in the book, many actors, directors, writers, and others connected with the industry suddenly discovered that their services were no longer needed. Among those who lost their jobs were Philip Loeb, who played Jake on the *The Goldbergs,* accused by *Red Channels* of communist sympathies for sponsoring an "End to Jim Crow in Baseball Committee." Banished from television and radio, he later died of a sleeping pill overdose. The blacklisting also led to many ridiculous, humorous incidents, such as the New York Yankees' refusal to allow catcher Yogi Berra to appear on a television show with blacklisted actor John Gilford, even though a Yankee spokesman asserted that Berra did not know "the difference between communism and communion."

Another major victim of the Great Fear was higher education. Communism in the United States had always drawn a large proportion of its followers and sympathizers from intellectuals, so it was not surprising that HUAC, state legislators, and other witchhunters would go after college professors. Many were deprived of their tenure, placed on probation, or fired for refusing to take state-imposed loyalty oaths, for taking the Fifth Amendment during investigations or trials, for holding unconventional opinions, for refusing to testify against their colleagues, or for signing petitions protesting violations of civil liberties by governments and vigilante groups. At the University of Minnesota, a black professor of philosophy who admitted to being a socialist and vice chairman of the Minnesota Progressive party was harassed by the administration and the FBI, subjected to unsubstantiated rumors that he was a homosexual and had engaged in sexual affairs with white female students, and finally dismissed by the administration for "lack of scholarly promise." At Kansas State Teachers College an economics professor lost his job for simply signing a petition urging the pardon of communists who had been arrested and imprisoned under the Smith Act.

By the time the Great Fear had run its course, six hundred college professors had been dismissed. No wonder many professors were afraid to discuss controversial subject matter, to subscribe to leftist publications, or even to be associated with liberal—much less socialist or communist—ideas, causes, or organizations. Understandably, most signed the loyalty oaths. Joseph Heller, an English professor at Penn State who was working on his novel *Catch-22,* probably spoke for many when he said that he regarded the oath "as an infringement of liberty, but it was only a tiny inconvenience compared with having no job."

The public schools, like the colleges and universities, also suffered from the Great Fear. All across the country public school educators were subjected to loyalty oaths, dismissals with or without a hearing due to real or alleged affiliation with radical groups, bans on the teaching of radical ideas, and scrutiny of teaching materials by local censors. This national crusade against communism in the schools was promoted by McCarthy and other politicians in

Washington, by state legislatures, by state and local politicians, by superpatriotic organizations like the DAR and the American Legion, and by books and mass magazines. In the October 1951 edition of *Reader's Digest,* for example, author John T. Flynn warned in "Who Owns Your Child's Mind?" that social science teachers were spreading socialist propaganda in the public schools and urged parents to get actively involved in the surveillance of the teachers and books that were molding the minds of their children. Hundreds of similar articles appeared in other magazines and newspapers, combining with rightwing books and pamphlets with titles like "How Red Is the Little Red Schoolhouse?" to spread the idea that subversives would capture the minds of the nation's young children unless parents and other concerned groups joined hands to fight the conspiracy.

Libraries were also favorite targets of overzealous patriots. In many cities, librarians were forced to purge from their shelves not just copies of the *Daily Worker or the National Guardian* but also of *The New Republic, The Nation, The Negro Digest, The Saturday Review of Literature, National Geographic, Look, Life,* and *Time.* Books by communist, socialist, liberal, or black authors were often pulled from the shelves, as were books and other materials critical of American capitalism, government, religion, or other American values and institutions or favorable toward the United Nations, disarmament, world peace, integration, interracial marriage, and even the fluoridation of city water supplies. Books on sex education or birth control were usually taboo, along with novels with obscene or suggestive passages. Sometimes it seemed that the censors were trying to outdo one another in the lengths they went to in trying to protect the public from "dangerous materials." In 1952, the Los Angeles Board of Education banned all UNESCO publications from the libraries and classes of the public schools, while in the winter of 1953 and 1954 one member of the Indiana State Textbook Commission tried to get books on Robin Hood expunged from the school curricula and libraries. His reason? The communists, he said, were trying "to stress the story of Robin Hood. They wanted to stress it because he robbed the rich and gave it to the poor. That's the Communist line. It's just a smearing of law and order."

The Great Fear often reached even more ridiculous dimensions. Indiana required professional wrestlers to take a loyalty oath, while the District of Columbia refused to issue a retailers license to a secondhand furniture dealer who had taken the Fifth Amendment when questioned about communism. In New York one town required a loyalty oath for a license to fish from city reservoirs, and in another a court granted a woman an annulment of her marriage on the grounds that her husband was a communist. In Cincinnati, the Cincinnati Reds' baseball club tried to demonstrate its Americanism by changing the club's name to the Cincinnati Redlegs; however, the fans rejected this change in the name of the nation's oldest professional baseball team, stubbornly maintaining, as sportswriter Tom Swope put it, that "we were Reds before they were." In Wisconsin, when the *Madison Capital-Times* sent a reporter out on the city streets on July 4, 1951, to ask passersby to sign a petition made up of quotes from the Declaration of Independence and the Bill of Rights, only one out of over a hundred people who examined the petition agreed to sign it. The others declined on the grounds that the ideas in the petition were communist, un-American, or in some other way subversive. Newspapers in New Orleans and several other cities tried the same experiment that year and obtained basically the same results. No wonder that a few months later, in January of 1952,

Claude M. Fuess wrote in a *Saturday Review* article on the temper of the times that "we are dominated by a fear so pervasive that it approaches hysteria."

Just how strong was the communist menace in America? Not very. Founded in 1919 after the Bolshevik Revolution, the American Communist party had always recruited most of its followers from a handful of urban intellectuals, idealists, and malcontents who joined the party because they were alienated from American society or saw communism as the best solution to the problems of American capitalism. The party had always suffered because of its close ties to Moscow, which made it seem like an agent of a foreign country, from its stigma as an alien ideology in a nation that was inherently suspicious of un-American isms, and from its own internal quarrels and power struggles. Furthermore, the weak class consciousness in the country robbed the party of its appeal to the working classes, labor unions, and blacks. Consequently, the party had always been only a minor irritant in American politics and communism a vastly overrated danger to the country's security. The communist presidential candidate William Z. Foster received fewer than 103,000 votes in 1932, when party leaders had expected the depression to bring them millions of followers, and his successor, Earl Browder, was able to garner only 80,000 votes in 1936 and some 46,000 in 1940. After this third loss to Roosevelt, the party did not even put forth its own candidates, supporting instead Roosevelt in 1944 and Progressives Henry Wallace in 1948 and Vincent Hallinan in 1952. Furthermore, not a single communist candidate for Congress ever got elected.

In terms of party membership, the party reached its peak during the days of Russo-American collaboration during the Second World War, when it numbered perhaps as many as 60,000 to 80,000 official members. But in the postwar period Russian aggression, the rise of the Cold War and arms race, government repression, and rapid growth of domestic prosperity combined to cause a dramatic decline in the party's fortunes. Party membership fell to 43,000 in 1950, to 10,000 in 1957, and to around 5,000 (including FBI agents and informers) in 1960, while the circulation of the party's organ, *The Daily Worker,* dropped drastically as well, falling from 23,000 in 1945 to 10,433 in 1953 alone. In 1959 David Shannon was able to write in his history of the party, The Decline of American Communism, that "at this moment, the Communist Party seems destined to join a collection of other sects as an exhibit in the museum of American Left Wing Politics."

Ironically, the greatest threat to American freedom in the fifties was not the communism that was feared by so many, but the spread of irrational anticommunism and the rise of right wingers and fascists who were willing to suspend civil liberties and other constitutional rights and freedoms in order to fight an overblown communist threat. As Truman and other critics tried to point out in the fifties, McCarthy and his type were the best friends the Soviet Union had in America, for they did much more to disrupt American foreign policy and domestic tranquility than American communists could ever hope to do. Truman was not just engaging in political rhetoric in his often-repeated assertion that "the greatest asset the Kremlin has is Senator McCarthy."

Justice Denied in Massachusetts

by Edna St. Vincent Millay

*In the 1920s two Italian immigrants, Sacco
and Vanzetti, were convicted of robbery
and murder on circumstantial evidence.
Many people believed that they didn't get
a fair trial because of their political beliefs.
Despite protests, they were electrocuted in
1927. This poem uses imagery to show
the damage done to society by wrongful
executions such as those in 1927 and
those in Salem in 1692.*

Let us abandon then our gardens and go
    home
And sit in the sitting-room.
Shall the larkspur blossom or the corn grow
    under this cloud?
Sour to the fruitful seed
5   Is the cold earth under this cloud,
Fostering quack and weed, we have marched
    upon but cannot conquer;
We have bent the blades of our hoes against
    the stalks of them.

Let us go home, and sit in the sitting-room.
Not in our day
10   Shall the cloud go over and the sun rise as
    before,
Beneficent upon us
Out of the glittering bay,

And the warm winds be blown inward from
    the sea
Moving the blades of corn
15   With a peaceful sound.
    Forlorn, forlorn,
Stands the blue hay-rack by the empty mow.
And the petals drop to the ground,
Leaving the tree unfruited.
20   The sun that warmed our stooping backs and
    withered the weed uprooted—
We shall not feel it again.
We shall die in darkness, and be buried in the
    rain.

What from the splendid dead
We have inherited—
25   Furrows sweet to the grain, and the weed
    subdued—
See now the slug and the mildew plunder.
Evil does overwhelm
The larkspur and the corn;
We have seen them go under.

30   Let us sit here, sit still,
Here in the sitting-room until we die;
At the step of Death on the walk, rise and go;
Leaving to our children's children this beauti-
    ful doorway,
And this elm,
35   And a blighted earth to till
With a broken hoe.

The Very Proper Gander

by James Thurber

James Thurber made a career out of poking fun at modern human beings and their complicated society. In this fable he uses a play on words to show how rumors, such as those that the girls spread in The Crucible, *can distort the truth.*

Not so very long ago there was a very fine gander. He was strong and smooth and beautiful and he spent most of his time singing to his wife and children. One day somebody who saw him strutting up and down in his yard and singing remarked, "There is a very proper gander." An old hen overheard this and told her husband about it that night in the roost. "They said something about propaganda," she said. "I have always suspected that," said the rooster, and he went around the barnyard next day telling everybody that the very fine gander was a dangerous bird, more than likely a hawk in gander's clothing. A small brown hen remembered a time when at a great distance she had seen the gander talking with some hawks in the forest. "They were up to no good," she said. A duck remembered that the gander had once told him he did not believe in anything. "He said to hell with the flag, too," said the duck. A guinea hen recalled that she had once seen somebody who looked very much like the gander throw something that looked a great deal like a bomb. Finally everybody snatched up sticks and stones and descended on the gander's house. He was strutting in his front yard, singing to his children and his wife. "There he is!" everybody cried. "Hawk-lover! Unbeliever! Flag-hater! Bomb-thrower!" So they set upon him and drove him out of the country.

Moral: Anybody who you or your wife thinks is going to overthrow the government by violence must be driven out of the country.

A Piece of String

by Guy de Maupassant

Guy de Maupassant is known for his realistic portrayal of French peasant life in the late nineteenth century and for his critical attitude toward human nature and society. In this story, set in the French province of Normandy, a man is falsely accused of a crime.

Along all the roads around Goderville the peasants and their wives were coming toward the town because it was market day. The men were proceeding with slow steps, the whole body bent forward at each movement of their long twisted legs, deformed by their hard work, by the weight on the plow which, at the same time, raised the left shoulder and swerved the figure, by the reaping of the wheat which made the knees spread to make a firm "purchase," by all the slow and painful labors of the country. Their blouses, blue, "stiff-starched," shining as if varnished, ornamented with a little design in white at the neck and wrists, puffed about their bony bodies, seemed like balloons ready to carry them off. From each of them a head, two arms, and two feet protruded.

Some led a cow or a calf by a cord, and their wives, walking behind the animal, whipped its haunches with a leafy branch to hasten its progress. On their arms they carried large baskets from which, in some cases, chickens and, in others, ducks thrust out their heads. And they walked with a quicker, livelier step than their husbands. Their spare straight figures were wrapped in scanty little shawls, pinned over their flat bosoms, and their heads were enveloped in white cloths glued to the hair and surmounted by caps.

Then a wagon passed at the jerky trot of a nag, shaking strangely, two men seated side by side and a woman in the bottom of the vehicle, the latter holding on to the sides to lessen the hard jolts.

In the public square of Goderville there was a crowd, a throng of human beings and animals mixed together. The horns of the cattle, the tall hats with the long nap of the rich peasant, and the headgear of the peasant women rose above the surface of the assembly. And the clamorous, shrill, screaming voices made a continuous and savage din which sometimes was dominated by the robust lungs of some countryman's laugh, or the long lowing of a cow tied to the wall of a house.

All that smacked of the stable, the dairy and the dirt heap, hay and sweat, giving forth that unpleasant odor, human and animal, peculiar to the people of the field.

Maître Hauchecome, of Breaute, had just arrived at Goderville, and he was directing his steps toward the public square, when he perceived upon the ground a little piece of string. Maître Hauchecome, economical like a true Norman, thought that everything useful ought to be picked up, and he bent painfully, for he suffered from rheumatism. He took the bit of thin cord from the ground and began to roll it carefully when he noticed Maître Malandain, the harness-maker, on the threshold of his door, looking at him. They had heretofore had business together on the subject of a halter, and they were on bad terms, being both good haters. Maître Hauchecome was seized with a sort of shame to be seen thus by his enemy, picking a bit of string out of the dirt. He concealed his "find" quickly under his blouse, then in his trousers' pocket; then he pretended to be still looking on the ground for something which he did not find, and he went toward the market, his head forward, bent double by his pains.

He was soon lost in the noisy and slowly moving crowd, which was busy with interminable bargainings.

The peasants milked, went and came, perplexed, always in fear of being cheated, not daring to decide, watching the vendor's eye, ever trying to find the trick in the man and the flaw in the beast.

The women, having placed their great baskets at their feet, had taken out the poultry which lay upon the ground, tied together by the feet, with terrified eyes and scarlet crests.

They heard offers, stated their prices with a dry air and impassive face, or perhaps, suddenly deciding on some proposed reduction, shouted to the customer who was slowly going away: "All right, Maître Authirne, I'll give it to you for that."

Then little by little the square was deserted, and when the Angelus rang at noon, those who had stayed too long, scattered to their shops.

At Jourdain's the great room was full of people eating, as the big court was full of vehicles of all kinds, carts, gigs, wagons, dump carts, yellow with dirt, mended and patched, raising their shafts to the sky like two arms, or perhaps with their shafts in the ground and their backs in the air.

Just opposite the diners seated at the table, the immense fireplace, filled with bright flames, cast a lively heat on the backs of the row on the right. Three spits were turning on which were chickens, pigeons, and legs of mutton; and an appetizing odor of roast beef and gravy dripping over the nicely browned skin rose from the hearth, increased the jovialness, and made everybody's mouth water.

All the aristocracy of the plow ate there, at Maître Jourdain's, tavern keeper and horse dealer, a rascal who had money.

The dishes were passed and emptied, as were the jugs of yellow cider. Everyone told his affairs, his purchases, and sales. They discussed the crops. The weather was favorable for the green things but not for the wheat.

Suddenly the drum beat in the court, before the house. Everybody rose except a few indifferent persons, and ran to the door, or to the windows, their mouths still full and napkins in their hands.

After the public crier had ceased his drum-beating, he called out in a jerky voice, speaking his phrases irregularly:

"It is hereby made known to the inhabitants of Goderville, and in general to all persons present at the market, that there was lost this morning, on the road to Benzeville, between nine and ten o'clock, a black leather pocketbook containing five hundred francs and some business papers. The finder is requested to return same with all haste to the mayor's office or to Maître Fortune Houlbreque of Manneville. There will be twenty francs reward."

Then the man went away. The heavy roll of the drum and the crier's voice were again heard at a distance.

Then they began to talk of this event discussing the chances that Maître Houlbreque had of finding or not finding his pocketbook.

And the meal concluded. They were finishing their coffee when a chief of the gendarmes appeared upon the threshold.

He inquired: "Is Maître Hauchecome, of Breaute, here?"

Maître Hauchecome, seated at the other end of the table, replied: "Here I am."

And the officer resumed: "Maître Hauchecome, will you have the goodness to accompany me to the mayor's office? The mayor would like to talk to you."

The peasant, surprised and disturbed, swallowed at a draught his tiny glass of brandy, rose, and, even more bent than in the morning, for the first steps after each rest were specially difficult, set out, repeating: "Here I am, here I am."

The mayor was awaiting him, seated on an

armchair. He was the notary of the vicinity, a stout, serious man, with pompous phrases.

"Maître Hauchecome," said he, "you were seen this morning to pick up, on the road to Benzeville, the pocketbook lost by Maître Houlbreque, of Manneville."

The countryman, astounded, looked at the mayor, already terrified by this suspicion resting on him without his knowing why.

"Me? Me? Me pick up the pocketbook?"

"Yes, you, yourself."

"Word of honor, I never heard of it."

"But you were seen."

"I was seen, me? Who says he saw me?"

"Monsieur Malandain, the harness-maker."

The old man remembered, understood, and flushed with anger.

"Ah, he saw me, the clodhopper, he saw me pick up this string, here, M'sieu' the Mayor." And rummaging in his pocket he drew out the little piece of string.

But the mayor, incredulous, shook his head.

"You will not make me believe, Maître Hauchecome, that Monsieur Malandain, who is a man worthy of credence, mistook this cord for a pocketbook."

The peasant, furious, lifted his hand, spat at one side to attest his honor, repeating: "It is nevertheless the truth of the good God, the sacred truth, M'sieu' the Mayor. I repeat it on my soul and my salvation."

The mayor resumed: "After picking up the object, you stood like a stilt, looking a long while in the mud to see if any piece of money had fallen out."

The good, old man choked with indignation and fear.

"How anyone can tell—how anyone can tell—such lies to take away an honest man's reputation! How can anyone—"

There was no use in his protesting; nobody believed him. He was confronted with Monsieur Malandain who repeated and maintained his affirmation. They abused each other for an hour. At his own request, Maître Hauchecome was searched; nothing was found on him.

Finally the mayor, very much perplexed, discharged him with the warning that he would consult the public prosecutor and ask for further orders.

The news had spread. As he left the mayor's office, the old man was surrounded and questioned with a serious or bantering curiosity, in which there was no indignation. He began to tell the story of the string. No one believed him. They laughed at him.

He went along, stopping his friends, beginning endlessly his statement and his protestations, showing his pockets turned inside out, to prove that he had nothing.

They said: "Old rascal, get out!"

And he grew angry, becoming exasperated, hot, and distressed at not being believed, not knowing what to do and always repeating himself.

Night came. He must depart. He started on his way with three neighbors to whom he pointed out the place where he had picked up the bit of string; and all along the road he spoke of his adventure.

In the evening he took a turn in the village of Breaute, in order to tell it to everybody. He only met with incredulity.

It made him ill at night.

The next day about one o'clock in the afternoon, Marius Paumelle, a hired man in the employ of Maître Breton, husbandman at Ymanville, returned the pocketbook and its contents to Maître Houlbreque of Manneville.

This man claimed to have found the object in the road; but not knowing how to read, he had carried it to the house and given it to his employer.

The news spread through the neighborhood. Maître Hauchecome was informed of it. He immediately went the circuit and began to recount his story completed by the happy climax. He was in triumph.

"What grieved me so much was not the thing itself, as the lying. There is nothing so shameful as to be placed under a cloud on account of a lie."

He talked of his adventure all day long; he told it on the highway to people who were passing by, in the wineshop to people who were drinking there, and to persons coming out of church the following Sunday. He stopped strangers to tell them about it. He was calm now, and yet something disturbed him without his knowing exactly what it was. People had the air of joking while they listened. They did not seem convinced. He seemed to feel that remarks were being made behind his back.

On Tuesday of the next week he went to the market at Goderville, urged solely by the necessity he felt of discussing the case.

Malandain, standing at his door, began to laugh on seeing him pass. Why?

He approached a farmer from Crequetot, who did not let him finish, and giving him a thump in the stomach said to his face: "You big rascal."

Then he turned his back on him.

Maître Hauchecome was confused. Why was he called a big rascal?

When he was seated at the table, in Jourdain's tavern he commenced to explain "the affair."

A horse dealer from Monvilliers called to him: "Come, come, old sharper, that's an old trick; I know all about your piece of string!"

Hauchecome stammered: "But since the pocketbook was found."

But the other man replied: "Shut up, papa, there is one that finds, and there is one that reports. At any rate you are mixed up with it."

The peasant stood choking. He understood. They accused him of having had the pocketbook returned by a confederate, by an accomplice.

He tried to protest. All the table began to laugh.

He could not finish his dinner and went away, in the midst of jeers.

He went home ashamed and indignant, choking with anger and confusion, the more dejected that he was capable with his Norman cunning of doing what they had accused him of, and even boasting of it as of a good turn. His innocence to him, in a confused way, was impossible to prove, as his sharpness was known. And he was stricken to the heart by the injustice of the suspicion.

Then he began to recount the adventures again, prolonging his history every day, adding each time new reasons, more energetic protestations, more solemn oaths which he imagined and prepared in his hours of solitude, his whole mind given up to the story of the string. He was believed so much the less as his defense was more complicated and his arguing more subtle.

"Those are lying excuses," they said behind his back.

He felt it, consumed his heart over it, and wore himself out with useless efforts. He wasted away before their very eyes.

The wags now made him tell about the string to amuse them, as they make a soldier who has been on a campaign tell about his battles. His mind, touched to the depth, began to weaken.

Toward the end of December he took to his bed.

He died in the first days of January, and in the delirium of his death struggles he kept claiming his innocence, reiterating:

"A piece of string, a piece of string—look—here it is, M'sieu' the Mayor."